CITY OF BONES

KWAME DAWES

CITY
OF
BONES

A TESTAMENT

TRIQUARTERLY BOOKS/NORTHWESTERN UNIVERSITY PRESS
EVANSTON, ILLINOIS

TriQuarterly Books
Northwestern University Press
www.nupress.northwestern.edu

Copyright © 2017 by Kwame Dawes. Published 2017 by TriQuarterly Books / Northwestern University Press. All rights reserved.

Printed in the United States of America

10 9 8 7 6 5 4 3 2

Library of Congress Cataloging-in-Publication Data

Names: Dawes, Kwame Senu Neville, 1962–
Title: City of bones : a testament / Kwame Dawes.
Description: Evanston, Illinois : TriQuarterly Books/Northwestern University Press, 2017. |
    Poems.
Identifiers: LCCN 2016036602 | ISBN 9780810134621 (pbk. : alk. paper) |
    ISBN 9780810134638 (e-book)
Classification: LCC PR9265.9.D39 A6 2017 | DDC 811.54—dc23
LC record available at https://lccn.loc.gov/2016036602

The paper used in this publication meets the minimum requirements of the American National Standard for Information Sciences—Permanence of Paper for Printed Library Materials, ANSI Z39.48–1992.

Contents

Part Two: Just Play the Damned Tune

Part Three: Reading the Sky

PART FOUR: CITY OF BONES

Acknowledgments

"Avery," "Avoiding the Spirits," "The Burden," "Creed," "Elevator," "If You Know Her," and "Thieving" were published as new works in *Duppy Conqueror: New and Selected Poems* (Copper Canyon Press, 2013), which received a 2014 Paterson Award for Literary Excellence and was a finalist for the 2014 Binghamton University Milt Kessler Poetry Book Award. Grateful acknowledgment is made to the following print and online publications, where certain poems in this collection, some in slightly modified form or with slightly altered titles, first appeared or were reprinted:

African Poetry Anthology, "News from Harlem," "What Ola Says"

The Baffler, "Equations"

Bengal Lights, "The Old Woman on the Road"

The Best American Poetry 2013, "Death: Baron Samedi" (published as "Death")

The Best American Poetry 2014, "News from Harlem"

Black Renaissance Noire, "If You Know Her," "The Old Woman on the Road," the "Iron" and "Flack" portions of "Psalm 104"

Hard Lines: Rough South Poetry, "Reburial," "Thief"

Harpur Palate, "Celebrity," "Trumpet"

Harvard Divinity Bulletin, "To Buy a Pair of Shoes"

Hayden's Ferry Review, "Black Suits," "News from Harlem"

Hunger Mountain, "Prelude," "Scent," "The Separation/Retention"

Jasper, "The Way of the World"

The Kenyon Review, "Making a Deal"

The Missouri Review, "Stop Time"

Narrative, "Avoiding the Spirits"

Narrative Northeast, "Before You"

The Normal School, "An Unfinished Life"

Oxford American, "Past Fifty," "Time," "Work"

Paterson Literary Review, "Making Love in a Boarding House," "Plot"

The Platte Valley Review, "Rose"

Plume, "Hitter," "What God Says"

Poet Lore, "Cross Burning," "Rose"

Poetry Daily, "News from Harlem," "Rope," "Steel"

The Pushcart Prize XXXVIII: Best of the Small Presses, "The Separation/Retention"

Rattle, "Rope"

The Southeast Review, "Mama Ola Speaks"

32 Poems, "Just Play the Damned Tune" (published as "Just Play the Damned Piece")

TriQuarterly, "Journeyman"

2 Bridges Review, "Spring," "The Things You Forget in Jail"

Verse Daily, "Death: Baron Samedi" (published as "Death")

Washington Square Review, "Mist," "Stillness."

The poems collected here represent the result of a long, ongoing conversation with the plays of August Wilson, with particular attention to *Ma Rainey's Black Bottom, Fences, The Piano Lesson, Joe Turner's Come and Gone,* and *Gem of the Ocean.*

This may seem a contradiction, but . . . it is neither a crime nor an absurdity. When we profess, as our fundamental principle, that liberty is the inalienable right of every man, we do not include madmen or idiots; liberty in their hands would become a scourge. Till the mind of the slave has been educated to perceive what are the obligations of a state of freedom, the gift would insure its abuse.

—George Washington to British actor John Bernard

Love in a hut, with water and a crust,
Is—Love, forgive us!—cinders, ashes, dust;
Love in a palace is perhaps at last
More grievous torment than a hermit's fast—
That is a doubtful tale from the faery land,
Hard for the non-elect to understand.

—John Keats, "Lamia"

Section 1. Neither slavery nor involuntary servitude, except as a punishment for crime whereof the party shall have been duly convicted, shall exist within the United States or any place subject to their jurisdiction.

Section 2. Congress shall have power to enforce this article by appropriate legislation.

—Thirteenth Amendment to the United States Constitution

PART ONE

Stealing Home

My ailing father
listening to the crickets
last day of August

—Rick Black

Crossroads

Lie down, lie down and live
As quiet as a bone
　　　　　—Dylan Thomas, "Once Below a Time"

Manning, South Carolina

This is the dark of Babylon, tawny
prairie lands dull with light snow,

the sky heavy with gloom; my mornings
continue the nightmare of cold eating

away at the wrack of my body; so
dry, so bleak, so complete. The Devil

is at the crossroads. Would have preferred
to meet my panting father, his eyes

so long emptied of hope—he couldn't
even get drunk right—how they made

him like this, his last dream blighted
by the thud on his flimsy wall,

the foreman's bark, the burden
of cotton; the truth that there is

nothing but a beast's emptiness
to his life, caged in the limits

of his district, caged by the rituals
of burying the dead long before

they have died, caged by the hunger
of children. Good God, even the nastiest

sinner knows not to go get drunk
in the steamed-up chapel where

Jesus promises a party in the here-
after. Wish it *was* my papa

with his big hands, with his
fistful of his fat dick asking

me if I have a problem if he
can taste some of my girl's cream,

maybe find his way to heaven
before I do, and he beat

me off her, dropped his overalls
and made her go mute in dust

beneath the towering elms, the horse,
scrawny as these bodies of ours

ritualizing the way a man becomes
a man. I had to whip him, had

to beat on him, had to make blood
come from my father's head, had to

watch him crawl up against a tree,
look at me, tell me he will never see me

no more, never feed me no more,
like it was the biggest relief of his life,

like he had been waiting all his life
to cut me off of him for good.

And that girl, gathering her things,
told me to stay and make it right.

She said it would be foolish to starve
over some country pussy. "It ain't

nothing," she said. "Just plain stupid
to think a nigger girl needs a hero,

like I ain't never been screwed
by Satan looking for some heaven

in this ragged edge of life." Wish
it was my daddy at the crossroads

waiting for me, but he wasn't there.
It was just the Devil, and he got

mad 'cause I wasn't scared of him,
and I told him to do his worst. What

can a fool do to me in this
cold place where everything is dark

and home don't have a sound
no more? So tired, dear God,

I am so damned tired deep
down in my bones; I am so

tired of walking hard, so tired
of walking through this Babylon land.

Death: Baron Samedi

First your dog dies and you pray
for the Holy Spirit to raise the inept
lump in the sack, but Jesus's name
is no magic charm; sun sets and the
flies are gathering. That is how faith
dies. By dawn you know death;
the way it arrives and then grows
silent. Death wins. So you walk
out to the tangle of thorny weeds behind
the barn; and you coax a black
cat to your fingers. You let it lick
milk and spit from your hand before
you squeeze its neck until it messes
itself, it claws tearing your skin,
its eyes growing into saucers.
A dead cat is light as a live
one and not stiff, not yet. You
grab its tail and fling it as
far as you can. The crows find
it first; by then the stench
of the hog pens hides the canker
of death. Now you know the power
of death, that you have it,
that you can take life in a second
and wake the same the next day.
This is why you can't fear death.
You have seen the broken neck
of a man in a well, you know who
pushed him over the lip of the well,
tumbling down; you know all about
blood on the ground. You know that
a dead dog is a dead cat is a dead

man. Now you look a white man
in the face, talk to him about
cotton prices and the cost of land,
laugh your wide-open-mouthed laugh
in his face, and he knows one thing
about you: that you know the power
of death, and you will die as easily
as live. This is how a man seizes
what he wants, how a man
turns the world over in dreams,
eats a solid meal and waits
for death to come like nothing,
like the open sky, like light
at early morning. Like a man
in red pin-striped trousers, a black
top hat, a yellow scarf
and a kerchief dipped in eau
de cologne to cut through
the stench coming from his mouth.

Open Spaces

After "Seeking," by Jonathan Green

1

Deep in the dank forest, you can smell
the salt and rot of the coast. A memory
of another shore returns familiar as shells

you see around the roots of the old-growth trees,
the sandy earth. Here, deep in the green,
you find shelter in darkness. A man

strips to his firm nakedness, washes clean
by the creek, burns old clothes, stands
in the muggy air, waiting for his skin

to dry before he dons his robes, starts
to dance, cursing out of him the din
of betrayals and hexes. He feels his heart's

chaos. He knows the language of the dead,
hears the old bones stirring on the calm seabed.

2

After the crowding of trees and bush, after
the heavy stench of bodies breathing in a dark

shack, after the heavy clouds hammer
hard on our heads in this storm season, after the barks

of hounds closing in, the report of gunfire
(the hunters and the hunted), after the fenced-

in breathlessness of this farm boy's fear,
he looks for the open fields of cotton. Dense

avenues frighten him. Avoid those, avoid
too the mountains too morose for laughter.

He finds peace in the sweet-smelling green
of fresh-mown ballparks, their order, how a voice
carries for yards without returning, everything clean

as a new morning before the body recalls
its weight. He seeks now the absence of walls.

3

This entanglement of limbs; in deep August,
everything grows dark with heat; the swamp
smells of rotting flesh and the stewing lust
of youth trying to return to the cramped
enclosure of all beginnings. From here
everything is shadow and ghosts. The body
going ahead looks familiar. You follow, stare
ahead, trying to make out the features muddied
by the dusk. For decades after, this will be
your constant nightmare, the fleeing form,
the question hanging over you, you dumbly
following, the bloody flesh underfoot, the storm
overhead, the distance between knowing
and constant fear, your soft heart hardening.

4

After you have broken your father with your hands,
killing is easy. The killing itself is hard—bodies
are solid things, they don't break easy, they stand
most blows, but eventually they grow weary,
give up, lose all their fight. It is the labor
that is hard, but to kill, the thought of it—
after you've heard your father beg, holler
for your mercy; after you have made him crap
himself for fear of you—that part is easy.
Just a matter of time before some fool
will walk into your rage and find no mercy
on the other side. It's just a matter of a tool
swung right, and death happens. In your head
it's like breathing, since everything's already dead.

5

The penitent can feel the silk of sweat
under his arms, the funk of manhood
after labor; he has already learned the beat
of desire, the clamor of hunger in his blood.
The penitent is pointed to the west
where the dense forests hoard deep fears
and the whoop of crackers beating their chests
at the blooding of deer, and sometimes the fears
of a wayward negro caught up in lies.
Deep in the forest, the elders say, you will
find your truth. This penitent learns to fly
over the overgrown paths, to stand still
and listen for the calm voice of God
in the wind, the markings in the sky like blood.

6

There is always someone in the shadows
ahead, slipping in and out of light.
The artist can lose his way in these groves
of ancient trees, circling back, trying to fight
the urge to return to the clearing. He looks
for light, the way rays break through
the babel of leaves and branches;
and soon there is only the dull blue
of peace where the shadow launches
into a dance of welcome. The artist
paints a spirit-filled green prayer, lost
in the consuming and unsettling bliss
of recognition, the canvas growing
into a pathfinder, the sun falling.

Hitter

You chop enough wood, handle cows and drag
horses, make a farm; understand the rhythm
of seasons; study the sky for each change
of wind to teach you whether your next
year will be lean with starving; take the blows
on your skin; learn to build a fence, dig
the hole, shape the timber into neat
cylinders to line for miles the limits
of your universe. Your body understands
the value of food; the falling that makes
you learn to stand firm, your thighs
clumps of sturdiness. Give me the piece
of shaped willow, let me hold it like
an ax and swing against the wind;
I can make a ball rise into the sky,
feel the breath of power through me,
this gift of callused fingers and the rhythm
of the wind lining up against me;
this is the art I learn in the dawn,
while my body heaves and settles
the swoop of the ax through the air
to find that growing wedge in the wood,
the efficiency of slaughter, the thorough
unheralded act of order: this is the art
of a hitter. All sound, the rhythmic thuds,
the cluck of chickens, the train's hooting,
the trucks grumbling towards the north,
eating out the highway away from these
moribund fields, the flat loud harmonies
of the dust-bowl church in the valley,
my child's persistent wail, the women
calling my name, the crude, unfettered

howl of a crowd finding something
to praise despite the hunger and fear—
all sound rests on my damp skin
like a blanket of dust, and when
the soft sweet spot finds the ball
rotating before me, as if charmed,
and when it lifts and is carried
beyond us all, there is a leap of the heart,
the reassurance we all must feel
to see a man's body working as it ought.

Spring

Locked up in Pittsburgh in April;
the gutters are thawing. You know
summer will stink like death,
and the time will stretch.
Sober now, you remember.
In April the clouds are still
heavy and there is so little light.

A big-armed black man misses
things when the month turns:
the scent of mown grass,
the sweet raw of hot dogs
boiling, stale sweat released
in humid changing rooms,
the white of dogwoods
against the sudden greening,
the clogged-up nose
making whiskey a healer,
the heavy scent of week-old
lard browning whiting,
the sharpness of mustard-
soaked pulled pork.

These are the things that brought
you here to do this time:
a woman's laughter,
the feel of a man's flesh
giving to the thrust of steel.

The Things You Forget in Jail

Mostly words that when spoken will soften
your chest, make you think of other mornings
ahead; you forget them slowly, but
the dull pale wood panels, the rust
in the hinges, the thick scent of old food,
men's crotches and heavy-duty cake soap:
they fill the space of words you once
had; these new words become
your music: *foot, sore, rat, booze,*
crap, shank, cigarette, runs, anything to make
you hard. Mostly the names of things
that grow without you: words of an old
woman in a gingham skirt catching
dirt and the leeching of prickles
and weeds; names she offered with
a pointed finger, then talking the name
in her fingers, she said, "Smell," and
you did, and you traveled to a place
that understands the sweet heave
of stomach waking up with hope;
gingko, magnolia, honeysuckle,
camellia, azalea, wisteria, the music
of mint, ginger root, garlic, sweet
onion; the texture of soil
steamed in crap, the sweet promise
of good earth; you forget that you
could walk through a forest and find
meaty mushrooms, or the flower
to fill your mouth with sweet petals.
Mostly, you forget that you have
forgotten until one day you look
at the callus in your palms

and ask yourself what you know,
and you know that you have
forgotten the curve of a woman's
belly, the iron funk of her thighs,
the tiny lumps on nipples; the light
in her fingers, the taste of her skin,
the slippery oil of her desire.
And you know you knew nothing
and this is the truth of your hopelessness
now—how much you have forgotten,
how much you must forget
to find peace with the body's need.

Stop Time

Stop time: There is a grunt in the gap.
Stop time: There is a head nod in the gap.
Stop time: There is a *hallelujah* in the gap.
Stop time: There is a shudder in the gap.
Stop time: There is a *well* in the gap.
Stop time: There is a hiccup in the gap.
Stop time: Got a foot shuffle in the gap.
Stop time: There is a bright light in the gap.
Stop time: There is a breath in the gap.

In the congregation, the rigid law
of time is shattered by that sudden
stop, that breaking of all order,
making someone stumble if they
don't know the path; making a body
wonder at the space left, the emptiness
sudden so, sudden so, sudden so.
In the congregation, in that moment
when the handclaps and shouting,
the crowded-in room, and the sweat
eat away at the talc, a body
finds itself in the gap, and this
dance that lifts a big clumsy
man to his feet, makes him
turn, makes him jump, makes
him holler *Everything,* louder
and louder, *Everything!* And here
in this chapel the world is held
in the cradle of a song, and for this
one moment he knows how to walk,

how to ride through the world, how stop
time is the music of our resistance,
and the song is the healing of all pain.

Stop time: There is a *praise God* in the gap
Stop time: There is a *hmmmm* in the gap
Stop time: There is a *Jesus* in the gap
Stop time: There is a *yes, suh* in the gap
Stop time: There is a *hmmmm* in the gap.

Man

Clean-headed men, men who sit in that easy
sprawl of ownership, loose pants bundled
fabric around the balls, jockeys so you see
the print of their dicks that have walked
through so many thick-grassed fields,
chopping as if that is all a dick is made
to do; men who have ritualized the sipping
of brown liquor; men who've turned fool
from chasing after fresh pussy; men
full of stories about being drunk, about
how they pissed themselves on the spot;
men who know the value of a woman
who lays out their starched drill pants and softly
laundered cotton shirts; men who slap
Old Spice on their faces after a smooth
shave; men who shake their heads and say,
"You don't know nothing about what I've seen,
what I've done, what I've been through . . .";
men who know that they are always
doing better than their sons-of-bitches
fathers who were bums, who drowned drunk
in Mississippi, who gave them nothing
but a fat thigh and a big nose, and that
hint of evil and shine in the hair; men not
scared of death but scared of dying;
men with arms still stone-hard, fists
black-knuckled with scars, men who will
take you out if you try; men who know
where their pistols lie at all times;
these men, in their fedoras, their
polished shoes, the Florsheims, burnished
with patience—the layers of Kiwi,

the soft wet cloth, the waterproofing
blackening, the whip of a dry rag,
the smiling gleaming of the toe,
the smooth manliness of the sides,
the quick dab of black over the scuffs;
these are the men we are talking
about. These are the men we learn
to loathe, these are the men whose sins
are legion, these are the men who kneel
at the altar, these are the men who count
the collection, these are the men who guard
the Lord, these are the deacon men, lately
saved, these fathers of many, these silent
keepers of secrets: these are the men we praise.

Two Plants

I plant these seeds among thickets
of plants whose names I do not know;
I dig quick and hard, turn the soil—
twisting pink worms purpling on their
topside dance in my handful
of dark loam, so rich, so damp,
so warm. I plow, I level, then plow
again, picking out stones, lumps
of cement, old spoons, rusted cans
and caked-up pieces of paper, I plant
these seeds despite the crowding
of vegetation whose names I don't
know. I wait for rain, wait for light
to break through the shadowing trees,
wait for a hint—for pale rubbery
green shoots, for the promise
of life, something that ruled
my days on the farm, my days
on somebody else's land; my days
counting the weeks, the months
before harvest, before this back-
breaking labor for the man.
One plant breaks out, loud, boisterous,
first, but crippled. It limps along,
always struggling to live, always
ugly, always loyal to the soil;
it is the broken creature, just living,
just living in the yard. The second
breaks soil fully made, grows
stiff-backed upwards, asks for
nothing and gets everything,
pleads for nothing, gets blessings;

this diabolic plant has forgotten
the touch of my fingers, scratching
the soil to make a bed. This too
is my seed. They will poison
me before I understand them,
before I understand me in them.

Order of Things

For Rose

When a voice brings order, you bow;
not because you have no choice,
when you have been a woman since
eleven years old, finding your food,
picking your clothes, braiding
your hair, being big woman, counting
pennies, planning like next year
is tomorrow; when you have to build
your own gate, see before and behind,
look out for yourself; when the story
stops with you, and your father
is a story you were told, your mother
is the strung-out, skin and bone,
broken-down woman who you feed
and bathe and build a fence around;
when nobody has been there to answer
to, when for years everything depends
on you; well, when a man, thick
necked, sinew armed, hard as nails,
seen the world, known the feel
of batons on his back, knows his mind
and the minds of people walking
towards him at night, when a man
like that looks in your eyes and tells
you, you the kind of woman, needs
a dress of class; you the kind
of woman need shoes of leather, soft
on your feet; you the kind of woman
shouldn't be worrying of tomorrow;

you the kind a woman should be
able to put your head against
his chest and weep, a deep weeping;
well, you will come to rest in that voice,
and you will start to say things like "a woman
needs a man to make her feel
like a woman." And when he pushes
himself in you, and shouts out
before falling soft and broken
on you, you will know you are the kind
of woman who can cherish a man
for what he gives you that you
never had before, never at all.

Before You

For Rose

1

Yes, we were country, lived in shotgun
shacks, where the road loses its way
to dirt and live oaks and all along
the way ancient cypresses, but we'd play
deep in the swamp, where Collins
built his still and made sweet peach
moonshine; that is where we made stories
to cherish in our hearts, a place to reach
for something warm, something to make
a woman remember the blood rush
in the head, singing and doing the shake
and stump to the blues; there in the bush
where she was that pretty thing, her eyes
soft with needing, her mouth full of lies.

2

Yes, we was country, but even a country
girl knows the power of her coochie,
how it could wake her without mercy
late at night because of the sweet mystery
of a dream, because of the scent
of burning tobacco in the air, the taste
of man; country, but I learned
the calming of liquor, how all haste
leaves the head, how big laughter

can rise off the skin like mist at dawn.
Country, but I was a fine believer
in the power of my waistline, the bone-
shifting sweetness of nights of blue air,
the juke joint where you let go all cares.

3

Before you, man, I didn't join no church;
before you, man, Bessie Smith was my girl;
before you, man, used to wear my skirt
hitched up high around my thigh, used to twirl,
show off my hairy legs, so men could think
of all that hair climbing up my thighs.
Before you, I told God to just wink
for a minute while I learned the soft sighs
of women; before you, man, there were
no fences, no gates, just a wide
road; before you, I used to swear
like a whore and dance, all wild
and loose; so don't think I have forgotten,
despite my new self: this good holy Christian.

4

Before you, man, I traveled, Lord, I traveled.
Every town from Mississippi to Pennsylvania
was a shelter and I found a place to revel
in the freedom and glorious regalia
of a queen girl, wearing silk and satin
and shoes so pretty they became a drug.
Before you, man, people called me Passion
or Fast Rose or Magdalene, who ain't any
better than any hard-dancing girl. I made men

weep for their mamas, made bad women
soft so they wanted to call me "best friend
for life—sweet sister," and be my mother hens.
Before you, I could run, man, but now,
'cause of you, this fast girl's taking it slow.

Man Smell

Close to the bullpen, where the dust hangs
in the chill air, if you take a deep
breath, and if you know what you smelling for,
you can smell man—that man
smell thick with promise, the man
funk floating up from the shadows
like the sweet blue scent before storms;
that man smell that leads from the caverns
under the bleachers, walls thick
as bunkers, dark corridors where
no woman goes except that woman,
Clarice, who's been sweeping and
mopping the leavings of men so long
she can't appreciate that man
smell like a ripe woman like me
does. I come here when the earth
starts to turn green and softy, and dog
crap lines the paths, and the flowers
jump out at you from every corner,
and the graveyards are crowded
with the winter dead; and people
crowd for warmth—good negro
folk, so full of excitement about
pitchers and hitters and the rusty
scoreboards, they forget everything
else; forget that they can't make
ends meet, they owe the shark,
and some two-timing girl has
wrecked their life. Me, I come
to smell that man smell, that sweat
and crust, that bitter cologne and grease,
that linseed oil and cheap liquor,

that dry sesame seed husks,
and that spit, so the place smells
like a farm, smells like crops
growing, the stink of man, that smell
that makes my stomach heavy,
makes me hold my head up
hoping for a right breeze to turn
the scent my way; call it a stink,
but it is the stink of our unholy temple
where we met, man; and that scent's kept me
tied up with you all these years,
it is the joy I can still taste in my
mouth if I let myself, that is what makes
me cry when I think of all the hurt
you have put on me, man.

Cross Burning

You can smell the kerosene and charred wood
a mile away. Over the slope of the earth
you can see the glow against the heavy
blue night. A part of you knows that you
should walk under trees and among
shadows, that the moon is not your friend;
you know you should keep the rumble
of voices at your back, keep the scent
of fire behind; but even the best
of us, our hearts full of curiosity,
want to see, want to stare at fear,
learn its language. You crest the hill,
and below are the scattering of bones
you know, the streets you know,
the roof of Oscar the blacksmith,
the roof you stood on, hands full of slate
and nails, the roof from which you
surveyed the land—so many black
folks building homes like hope, and
the church said, "Sweet Jesus, oh
Sweet Jesus!" And the chicken
was sweet, the tea a comfort, the boot-
leg in the back making us mellow,
and this is how family grows
in the skin. But you can see
that flaming cross wilting the wild
flowers at the edge of the hill,
these white hoods of bodies stumbling
over uneven ground; you hear the sharp
crack of a rifle, and you see people,
casual as a Saturday night's fair, just
looking, chatting, spitting, searching,

laughing. Over in the woods behind
the house, you know a family is running,
trying to make it to the open road
by the river; you know a man
is broken, a woman is lamenting
and children are terrorized. Everything
is left behind, and the church is singing,
"Jesus, Jesus, Jesus!" You will walk
away from this, keep light at your back,
walk northward; your heart thick
with a simple truth about white folk;
it is the way you were made. ⌐

Plot

for Troy Maxson

A man must build a fence around life.
A man is an ordinary thing—flesh and bones.
A man screws his wife; there is love here.
They make babies. These creatures
crap, cry, grow, eat; can make a man
smaller than he imagined. Love, too.
A man can collect on the misfortunes
of his brother—that is the silence
of God. If you sin once, you can
smell the sulfur in the air, you see
the glow of damnation in the eastern
sky; and the train picks up speed.
But night falls, then day arrives
and God has not arrived. You sin
twice and it slips down your throat
like syrup, and you know that this
need to laugh, this hunger for a woman's
need—her need for your skin,
for the force of your body, this lie
she tells every day of the gloom
before you come—is God's gift,
the thing he knows you need
for being a good man, a chipped
and rusty man, but a there-are-worse-
men-than-me man. Sin seven times
and you don't know the meaning
of words. You tell the open sky
while you are walking homeward,

your body still tender from her greedy
devouring, you say, "This is a hymn
of praise; only the mighty could build
bodies for such sweetness." A man
wants to have the calm of home,
the order of silences; a man wants
obedient children and the grace
of heaven to say, yes, this last bit
of sweetness, this way your erections—
such precious things now—are not
wasted in the death of disinterest,
this rescuing of the last desire,
the last memory of manhood—
this too is God's gift. The plot
will shatter order, the wife will
know the truth, the mistress will grow
pregnant, and the sons and daughters
will lament the sins of their father.
This is the way a story is told. All we have
are the quick sparks of laughter along the way.

Rose

If you walk far enough into the hills,
far enough from the factory of smoke,
far enough from the garbage dump;
if you take a woman along those
tree-full streets, just where the village
center can't be seen, and you stand
under tree shade and look down
to the rivers and the bridges where
everything looks clean, and the city
is growing like somebody's feeding
it hope; and the boats float across
the surface of the river, peaceful;
if you take your woman so far
from it all, you will first smell
yourself, smell the sweet rot
of garbage so thick around you
most days you don't even know
what it smells like, you will smell
the trash in your skin and the cooking
sweat in your armpits, the funk
in your crotch, and you will know
that though she agreed to come
walking with you, she will smell
you and nicely tell you where to get
off; she won't say it, but she will
show you that you are out of your
league, outclassed, that you are just
a big-handed garbage man, a felon,
a damned has-been baseball player,
and you smell like crap. So you say
to her, gruff with shame, "I know
I smell like crap, but it is the work I do—

I move crap, it is what I do . . ."
And if she looks you in the eye
and says softly, "You don't smell
like crap, mister, you smell like work,
like a man should, and forgive me
for being so bold, but that is the sweetest
smell this girl knows in the world,"
you will feel to cry right there
for this pretty woman, this lady
who could never seem more precious
than she does now. And you will say to her,
"Well, baby, all I can smell on you
is pure roses, baby, sweet roses."

What God Says

In the same way, the husband's body does not belong to him alone
but also to his wife.
　　　　　—1 Corinthians 3:4

What you don't know is that when you lay
out on your back, sweet with good liquor
as you like to call it, and your face goes
slack, every strain to be the man drained
from your forehead, and I pull off your boots,
the socks with the hole in the right instep
that I have darned already and will again,
and then undo those buttons on your trousers,
untangle the belt and pull down those trousers—
heavy as the five-year-old I cradled in my arms—
full of coins, your knife, bundles of paper
wrapped with blackened cord, when I strip
off your shorts, then unbutton your shirt,
pulling you to one side then to the other
to take your arms out of the sleeves,
then dragging that cotton shirt, stained
under the armpits yellow, over your head,
to leave you laid out there like I know
you will be that day when Palmer will wash
you to fix you up with his chemicals
and paste and makeup—Palmer, who
will not know every fold under your chin,
or the way that long vein crawls over
your thick arms down to your wrist,
Palmer and his people, who don't know
the shape of your chest, hard at the top
and soft around these nipples you pretend
you don't like me to suckle on like a baby—

even though I can feel the nudge of your dick
every time I do—folks who won't know
every dark spot on your skin, the islands
of scars over your wide belly stretched tight
over the ropes of muscles barely visible
beneath the flesh, folks who don't know
to find the cluster of dense hair on your
left shoulder, who won't know what it is
to lay hands on you like a prayer, say, "Man,
God say all of this, all of this is mine.
Every inch of skin, every hair is mine."
They won't know what I know when I place
my hand under your scrotum and feel
the animal of you grow hard, grow to the shape
I know, each swell, each vein, each
wrinkle and blemish; and me saying,
"Even this, man, is mine." Even
when I can smell the funk of another woman
in your skin, even when I know *you* don't
know that it is all mine, even then,
I still stand over you, place my hand over
your chest and put my face against your face,
feel the breath of you on me; and in this
silence, I say to you, "Man, this is mine,
and, today, I won't take it away from you.
Today, I won't cover your slack face
with this pillow, because of love, man,
because of love, and because God says."

Creek

Before light, I drag the canoe down
the slick uneven slope. The air is heavy
with heat, already the hum of flies
dancing around the bald cypresses.
The creek is black, slippery, whispering
where the fallen trees clogged the stream.
In this soft morning, the world
belongs to the open sky. Even the old
folks, still drunk from Friday night's
libations, have not stirred. This
is where a girl will find herself,
find the secret in her heart, find
even those memories she has buried,
the anger, the desire, the tepid
mix of lust and fear. The canoe
slips out; I dip quietly, pulling
the paddle out smoothly, no splash,
just the slippage of a boat along
the creek. I lie on my back,
stare at the opening sky
and register this full silence,
the shelter of being alone like
a child hoarding her salvation
to come where the river bends.

Détente

Then one day you know you do not believe
your own threats; you know that the mystery
of your wisdom is a lie, and you feel
like a fool staring him down, telling
him he must do as you say. You know
he doesn't have to, you know he will call
your bluff. You stand there looking
at him and you both know you have
nothing left, short of killing him.
And even then, he will fight back,
his body will take a blow and reshape
itself for more. All you have is bluster,
words, and your two long arms;
all you have is the guilt you hope he feels.
This is your son, this man,
this scowling fool who hates
you like you have never known
hate, who is thinking, you know,
of stepping in your chest, stomping
you down, like you did your own
father, who cried like a baby,
crawling to the shelter of the live
oak, spitting blood, pleading
for mercy; and in that moment,
he broke something in you, killed
that last abiding myth, the fence
around you. You tell yourself
he must never feel alone like that,
abandoned like that; no son of mine
must think of the world as bleak
as you did that night, walking
east like you was looking for Africa,

leaving behind the homestead,
the bed, the order of things, alone
now. You stand here now,
waiting to tell a lie, waiting
to build a fence around you,
waiting like all fathers should.

Work

Five days to go: Working for the next day
—Bob Marley, "Work"

Look at this man's hands, look
at the toughness in his fingers,
the way his nails darken at the edges,
the way his skin is marked
by old scars, the way his palms
are leather-tough—a grater of skin
if he drags those palms over
your arm. Those hands still
remember the smooth shape
of wood, the grooves where
the blisters would settle and then
harden to toughness; the handle
of the clumsy seed planter, bouncing
on the uneven grooves, planting,
planting. Sometimes it is easy
to not know that on the plantation,
out there on James Island,
every morning, seven days a week,
a bell would sound out, and that
bell would mean that thirty minutes
was left before you lined up
by the fields to start to sweat.
And you would work all day
to pay rent on that wood shingle
and mud chimney that they
had given you. And if you missed
a day, your family would lose
shelter. That is work. Work is
keeping the wolves from your door,

work is the left foot following
the right, the sickle swinging,
the dirt on your skin. Work
is always being behind, always owing
somebody something. Work
is payment in June for debt
from last December, when the cold
reached into your gut, held
you down. Work is one pair
of shoes all season—barefoot
grown man all summer long,
and mules for the freeze
all winter. Work is the day
you think you are grown enough
now to run, to run from this
constant falling back, only
to find that big-bellied white
man with a shotgun saying, "Here are
some stripes, nigger, nice stripes
to help you work better—now
you get three meals a day;
now you get a bed to sleep on,
boy; now you got something
to live for." Work is all
a nigger has for sure, and work
tells you that nobody, nobody
is going to give you something
for nothing; work is like breathing—
and every breath is a loan
that you can never pay back.
Work is all a man has,
and work is nothing, nothing
at all; every day is work, work, work.

What's Left

A woman can take the things you long
for most; the thing that makes you feel
like his world would be grey without
you. When you see the jaunty swagger
in his step, and laughter comes off
him easy as water; when you can
tell that those fingers have grown
soft for someone else, it makes
you mourn what you have lost,
makes you start to count what
you have, hoarding it like you know
that with time it won't be yours.
When a man tells you he won't
give up that woman, when he
says he can't walk away from her,
you understand the world has stopped.
Once he became the softest
gift—those baby-producing years
full with bloat, tears and the flesh
of new life—how tenderly he cared
for you, crowded you with impossible
presence, held himself above you,
stroking you with the concentration
of a man intent on keeping safe
this precious thing; and how he howled
your name, so full of his man self
in the dark. That is the last gift
you will lose to that woman. And you
know that the news of her
pregnancy is the news of your death.

She will take it all from you;
leave you with lies, with title deeds,
with transacted wealth, with the cold
calculation of mammon.

Constancy

After a while the constancy of days
is our comfort. When a woman has
tasted good liquor, knows the giddy
euphoria of tumbling into the blur
of laughter, fresh weed and the warmth
in the skin of desire; when after
she has howled, "This is so good;
let me just die here like this," before
she passes out drunk with pleasure;
even after she has woken in a
web of lost memory and the ordinariness
of the lump of man beside her,
ready to plant his fist in her face,
ready to call her bitch; when
she has understood that what she
called love was a demon child
gestating in her womb for years,
growing fat, thick-skinned
and with hardened fingernails,
a rugged face of stubble,
a body too large for the sac,
heavy, gruff-voiced, squatting
at the base of her spine,
grumbling all the time for more
food; when she knows that to push
this overgrown thing out of her
will rip her body apart forever,
cause blood, cause flesh to rip;
when she has bled out the bloated
annoyance called love, leaving
herself broken, uncertain, and pained
with the strain, she finds comfort

in the ritual of a consistent
man, an ordinary man—and day
by day this constancy, this
ordinary gift, will turn into
something more, something she
is willing to give it all for—
and this is when a woman is
softest, when she stops looking
for the shock of rupture.
To shatter it all here is an act
of supreme cruelty; it is.

Demobbed

The man standing in the open field
holding a trumpet in his hand
is a soldier who has forgotten most
of what horn blowers play, his ear
shot to hell by the concussion
of bombs; and where his brain held
memory, a nest of shrapnel has settled
painlessly in the sap, thick, inert.
Tomorrow he will leave the coast,
discarding the dog tags, the boots,
the fatigues, the belts, the beret,
the canteen, the helmet all along
the highway, until, somewhere at
the edge of Pennsylvania, he is
down to the basics, a light bag
of papers, a sack for the horn,
and a head empty of everything
he has seen. Now we are told
we may be entertaining angels
unaware; here he comes, skipping.

Journeyman

1

The old jazzman at the Crawford Grill sits
at back of the club, three o'clock
in the day, just killing time. He spits
on the sun-cooked concrete. "Hell,"
he says, "look at that." He points
his chin to the stain of moisture
quickly drying until just a faint
stain remains. "We ain't here forever,"
he says. "You see the crap—gone
like that. Every song you sing
got a minute to live, then its done—
nothing left. You dead and ain't nothing
left." I know it's about this thankless art,
about my fingers on keys, about my heart.

2

Here is a good day—steak and eggs
and a mess of beans, a jug of coffee
and your crotch bruised sweet, the fat leg
of a woman sleeping by you, her reverie
a sign of the hard work you've done
to knock her cold. The slant of sunlight's
through the window while a soft hum
of rain calms the world; and last night
the music you turned out made people
weep, tears streaking big men's faces,
women drunk with nostalgia mumbling,

48

"Take me home, baby. Take me to places
I ain't been for a long while." The sweet aftermath
of perfection: even when you know it won't last.

3

Yes, me too, I stood there on Wylie—the rivers
like a postcard behind—and watched that ball,
still grey, cut a slow flight through air to shatter
the Crawford Grill; three stories: the grand hall,
Crawford Club where the big-shot black folks
would pretend they owned the world. No sound
but the grumble and clatter of concrete,
and, like they say, when all is said and done,
there is nothing left but dust, broken streets,
some liquor talk, and every magic music
that crowded those rooms night after night
has gone; lost for good. I kept me a brick
which I put to my ears, just so I might
hear me playing with sweet Billy Eckstine
the night he smiled and called me King.

4

Crawford Grill, Hurricane Lounge, Savoy Ballroom,
Musician's Club: catch me on a Saturday
night, Lord, the Hill is jumping; take a broom
and sweep negroes up them stairways,
and find a woman with meaty strong calves,
big ass and a sweet mouth; everything is sticky
with funky jazz, and down-South blues, tough
as a convict's hands; man, we dance, sweaty,
loose, crazy, and people know my name;

call me by my name. This is my church,
and come Sunday, I am broke; no more game.
Just take me by my old man, where I perch
on his porch, waiting for his scathing
and worthless pity, his grudging blessing.

Celebrity

For Charles Harris

Here go the Crawford Colored Giants. Take
my picture, Mr. Teenie; you know I could
make you a star; could make it that
you don't have to run numbers no more;
just catch my big smile and pass it
along; make me look good, that's all.
When I swing that tree trunk, I will
always smile so people will know
this man playing with other men
like they are boys. Here go Satchel
Paige. Man's one ugly fellow, but Lord,
he learned to make everybody
else laugh so hard they look
ugly like him. Here go Josh Gibson;
ask him to tell you who everybody
said was the hardest-hitting,
cleanest-eyed nigger up there in
Pittsburgh; ask him to tell you
what he said to the devil down
there by the Ohio River, under a bridge,
drunk us a skunk, what he shouted
into the winter sky after he puked
two days of barbecue and bourbon
into that river—how he told Scratch
to make a deal, give him Old Troy
Maxson's quick eye and cold swing
and he'd be glad to settle down
in a duplex in hell. That is what
he said, crying like that, and we all

heard it, Mr. Teenie. So folks
know that what you see ain't
all there is. This fat rolling man,
big hands, big head, a belly
taut like he got seven months of child
in him; this piece of everyday
shit who can't get no respect
from his own offspring, who
moves other people's shit
for a living; this simple black man
used to be somebody, Mr. Teenie,
so take the damn picture. I could
make you famous, brother, you know it.

She

1

It is not hard to see the beauty of youth,
the heavy defiance of breasts, as if planted
there, the smooth innocence of sparse growth
over her curved belly, the back slanted
just so, and the casual bounce of her ass.
A man's palms long for the push back
of flesh, the easy journey down her flank,
the laughter, the surprise of her slack
weight—things she knows; she even thanks
him afterwards. She, the usurper of all
I have; she, the fertile ground, where seeds
sprout wildly; she of giggles, the spoiler,
the one who understands her power
that tight pussy, smooth-faced overthrower.

2

You know she is sweet as a daughter,
you know when her periods come she cries,
curls up and asks him to come cover
her with blankets and collect her soft sighs;
you know she fixes him meals she knows
his mother used to make; makes him eat
while she looks at him smiling; you know
she smashes plates, crosses her chest, beats
him with her fists, letting him hold her back,
laughing at her flame, and she falls
into his arms, weeping so he smacks

her ass, tells her to hush soft-soft, all
tender, till she calls him Big Daddy Troy.
She opens to him, giggling, "Come, big boy."

3

You loved me most when I was swollen
with these babies, when I was a waddler,
when my stomach churned, my body stolen
by them, when I was so fat. Under
all that water and flesh, you loved me,
man. You rubbed my feet, pressed big
hands into my back till a slippery
finger tested my wet; you used to sing
to me, pushing in so slow, asking,
"You okay? You okay?" And how tender
you were, holding yourself back, humming
until I shuddered onto you, remember?
You loved me then like a gardener
of delicate things, my sweet, sweet lover.

4

When a man says his sin is his life,
and though caught, he won't let go
of the bitch; when he says to his wife
he wants to stay, but she has to know
that he will continue to take the girl
on the side, and pay for her panties,
and eat her food; what in the world
is a woman to do? She will try pleas
for love, loyalty, decency, but soon

she will grow a stone in her belly,
and a callus over her heart, then bloom
bitterness so thick and smelly
to darken and stink up this nest.
She will then become a deep forest.

Debt

What is owed us, our bodies slumping
from years of labor, the promise of longevity
a lie? We cannot count the years
like others; so we flame in those
early years when our bodies are reliable,
when our strength can let us be
beaten, used; and we bounce back
bellies full of laugh, fists swinging:
this is all it is. At forty, we are
limping, the calculation is basic,
ten more years if we are lucky.
These are the times to make amends
for the wounds; we learn to cry,
learn to say, "Don't leave me," learn
to drink in the dark, feel the rumbling
of death; learn to stare
at a wall for hours, to know
how comforting this emptying
of the brain can be, this silence,
how memory, played out in such
silences, can soothe. What is owed
this man with big arms, useless
shoulders, and dick that has
forgotten its own nature, a man
who has lived on the edge
of grand things; what is owed
him but his daily wage for
his labors, a safe path to walk
each day, the right to gather as a man
among men, get drunk, sleep it off
and stare at walls, counting the days?

She is dead, the girl who carried
his seed; he has broken her. How happy
he was to see her glow with the swell
of the child in her, and then the way
she slipped away, a mattress soaked
in blood, the baby, the girl wailing,
his hands too clumsy to hold this
flesh, what is owed an ordinary
black man with nothing to show
for his life? In the dark, the wounded
wife plants geraniums and sings
hymns in the dark-loamed garden,
the infant girl giggles in the sunlight,
the earth turns slowly. He allows
the blanket to cover him, travels
to the open lot of a ballpark, dust
dancing in the air, a clean sky
and the scent of mown grass—
this is all he is owed today.

Trumpet

Before the dance in the dusty yard;
before old issue army boots that smell
like France, worn to flapping tongue,
cracked sole and laceless looseness
have stumped the ground, making
the rhythm that reaches deep into
the art, the throb of music for
drunk ancestors; before his bone-
and-muscle legs start the last
shuffle and leap of a man who
has collapsed unto his uncertain
madness; before he arrives at this
doorway at the end of a dream,
this doorway leading to the absence
of knowing, of answers; before
he arrives here in the glaring
silence of a Pittsburgh July day,
the screaming and concussion
of the 4th now distant, the flies
traveling in droves coloring the world
black; before he understands
the sadness of this fenceless
house where the dead man's
body is laid on the dining
table, where the widow stands
in elegant black, the bones of her
cheeks sharp as stoic grace, her
face dry, no tears—this shadowed
woman waiting with long glasses
of cool lemonade; before the son's
return, prodigal and broken, a soldier
who has stared into redness

of exploded bodies before
this play finds its truest music,
the headlong rush to meaning,
to redemption, for mercy, oh mercy;
before all this, the man with
a plate of metal stitched to his
skull raises the cornet to his lips,
blows, blows, blows until
the impotence of his breath
whooshes out into the silence.

Hope's Legacy

1
Cory Maxson

I had perfected the exquisite hatred;
it took little: the metallic taste of neat

bourbon, the thought of someone taking the heat
for someone else, or the word "father,"

and I was awash in its logic. Now
you are dead and even this dry fodder

of memory won't catch for long. How
it sputters, then dies! Emptied of you

I have no one to hate; my long arms
weigh me down. You remember old Blue,

the dog you loved? He hated your stories,
but when you died he howled, 'cause he knew;

and I let him tremble in his sorrows,
but after, he loved me next, without a fuss.

2
Rose Maxson

A part of you will never grow soft,
not the moment he chose her instead
of you, not the knowing of what you lost
by faithfulness, how you left as dead

the hunger to dance, drink whiskey,
laugh—just for love. Those parts
will never soften, but there are memories
that won't grow into stone; the heart
understands its recollection of first things.
The loss, the still warm hand
on your back, the tears while he came
roughly in you, weeping man,
saying, "Love, love, love," and the same
softness will keep you to see this child,
growing innocently, running so wild.

3
Lyon Maxson

Maybe climbing that last hill, seeing the shadow
of the house with the wide gaps in the fence
and the old man holding forth, talking slow,
the joke growing fat with lies; maybe, tense
and nervous for a minute, I will wonder
if this time I will leave with lint in my pockets,
with the shame of his bullying, the thunder
of his curse shaking me again; and yet
somehow, deep down, I know that though
he calls me a waste of sperm, a dreamer,
a fool, a boy with only music to show
for it all, he will still call me in closer;
laughing, he will say my name softly,
give me some money, and even hold me.

4
Jim Bono

Thank you, friend, for your spectacular faults;
even strangers call me saint for my silence

beside you; the preacher warned me of bolts
of lightning missing you, flaming the wrong man.

Thank you; even my woman thinks me pure
because of your glorious doggish splendor,
and my sins seem so small in your shame
I have gotten away with murder—

only Jesus seeing it all. I will miss you,
my captain, miss how you lead me
to my laughter, how you would never go
leaving me without a fence to keep me
safe, to let me know home; but now
I am naked; the world's grown dark, slow, slow.

5
Raynell Maxson

First, born with the flesh, a shelter,
breaking away, you, of blood and water,
arrive plump and loud in the swelter
of August. You are without mother
and a frightened father holds you, but you
have the love of Mercy, a woman
who takes you in, teaches you the blues
and the lift of hymns, builds a fence
about you, hovers over you with wings.
You are mothered when your father dies;
you are adored for your laughter; you sing
and dance; you make this woman smile
when she cries; you are the art of forgiveness;
you teach the wounded how to bless.

Time

1

All these shining things—the clean road,
long slick cars zipping, got steel, oh steel,
such shining new things—cover up the blood
they are spilling in Alabama. Girl, I feel
what you feel deep in the woods looking
at the hole in his socks, his big toe
sticking out; nothing shining here, nothing
beautiful, no, just the dry blood. Lord, show
my people who are grinning about how far
we've come, got white folks dancing
to some nigger singer—like this is where
we always wanted to go. Just these shining
things to blind us, tomorrow I will pick
them up on the roadside, no more slick.

2

We are at the edge of the madness,
sitting and swelling warm under the skin,
so you think that shuffling and press
of bodies against the fence will end?
You think the wail of that trumpet's
dizzy zigzag over the tracks, leaping
off the tracks, doing its own junk,
not giving a damn about lining
up to something set out: you think
this is where we are going? Listen,
hear the chaos of that drum stinking
up the joint; we are crazy, brain missing;
that screw they put in, it's gone, man,
and this madness is where all peace done gone.

Creed

Berniece don't believe in nothing. . . . She believe in anything if it's
convenient for her to believe.
　　　　　　　—Boy Willie, in *The Piano Lesson*, by August Wilson

She knows what comes with believing in God;
then you have to believe he is not a kind
God, and you have to believe he hates black
folk, and you must believe he could have
stopped Crawley from going out that night
to get shot by those white people over some
firewood—that's what comes from believing
in God. You believe in God, and you wonder
who's listening to you at night when
you let a man move on you, and then
you know he won't be back; you believe
in God, you will hope he comes back,
and you will be disappointed always
because he won't be back, he never
comes back, and where is God then?

She knows what comes from believing in ghosts
or spirits walking the path. If she does
that, she has to wonder if that smell
of her husband's sweat late at night
is him coming by to stay with her, and
then she has to wonder why he never comes
when she needs him; she will have to wonder
what all those old folks and younger boys,
who had to eat their own dicks while
hanging from a tree with these crackers
looking on, what are they singing now?

How can anyone believe they can hear those
voices? What kind of noise would that be?
She knows what comes from believing in
the rumors of trains filled with the lost
souls roaming around with the hunger
for vengeance. If you think this, if you
carry this, you can't go on, you can't
live like the world is in what you can
carry in your hands. What do you do with
your back, how you make things happen
on your own? Have nothing given
to you and nothing is taken from you.

She knows why she can't believe in nothing,
why she can't believe in prayer, 'cause
praying is to weep, praying is to beg,
praying is to throw your hard body
against the night because you have
nothing else. Music is a lie, music
will make you soft, will take you
away from the things you can hold
in your hands; music, those songs, that
sound, will wash you, make you fall
apart with nowhere to go. No, a woman
must believe in nothing, and nothing
will take her on. This is how you make
your world small enough for you
to wake up each morning and breathe.

PART TWO

Just Play the Damned Tune

Past Fifty

Put three fifty-year-old black musicians
in a studio in 1924, and you know by the numbers
that they were born so close to the stench
of slavery that they still smell it whenever it rises
from some broken-down black man's armpits
and crotch; they know their smell. Three
bluesmen, two can't read, never had to read
to make their big old hands turn those strings
into a symphony of rhythm and blues.
These three men haven't forgotten to always
look behind them wherever they go, always
study the shadows in a dark club,
always walk the wide-open roads;
and every one of them has a satchel
full of memories that have sat there
so long they come out as lies, or the
weight of silence when they aren't careful.
Take these fifty-odd-year-old negroes,
ask them to tell you about the blues,
and they will tell you about what cotton
feels like in your hand when you bleed
to pull it off the stems; they will
tell what it feels like to climb up
the wide trunk of a live oak tree,
crawl along the bolt-straight
lower branch to cut the rope
with the flies swarming your
face so the body of your cousin
could fall into the arms of the women
who will wash his skin, clean
the shit from his legs, and the spit

from his face, before they lay him out
on the table, singing hymns, wondering
why so many boys have to die
to the whoop of rebels, the thick smell of tobacco
and the circling of ghosts. Ask them
about the blues, they will tell you
about the taste of bile in your throat
when you are running through the night,
the sound of hounds at your back, and
you praying to make it to the bridge,
to familiar paths where you know
you will find shelter. Who is chasing?
Always hellhounds, Jesus, fired
up with moonshine and the hankering
for blood. The blues—that is rumors
of the Promised Land, that is the scattering
of the children of perdition along the dusty
roads of these southlands, nobody looking
back to see the smoke and flame over their
churches, their homes, their cities.
Ask them about the blues, they will
tell you what the train sounds like
as it comes through Mississippi, Alabama,
Arkansas, South Carolina, Georgia;
how it sounds as it takes you where
you have never been, and you always
looking back to see if they are still
coming for you. Ask them what is
the blues, and they will tell you it's that one
night when you can smell the remnants
of charcoal and barbecue sauce in the air,
and the low funk of spilt liquor
and cigarette ashes, and you feeling high
enough to know your name, and a woman
holds you so close you feel at last
that you can cry like the day your mama

held you, and you cry everything you have
out, and she takes you in, calls out your
name, pats you on your back, and sings
a song so sweet it has to be the blues.
A woman with no name somewhere
on the road, that is the blues, the comfort
of love, the weight of tears; just something
passing you by. Something makes you think
that the man coming to find you—the cracker
with his brothers and his shotgun—
'cause you owe him and, yes,
you owe him money because you figured
you could borrow money and pay it back,
because when you walked up to him
you felt like a man, and you felt strong,
and you felt there was no way you
couldn't pay him back like you said
you would, and now you don't have it,
and he won't wait no more—that feeling
making you think that running is
the only answer—the world passing
you by, happiness slipping away.
You don't live to be fifty-something
by fighting nobody that could
beat you up. You don't live to be
fifty and still be a negro man
by saying what is in your head
like that is freedom or some such shit.
You don't get to be fifty and still
standing by looking like you know
what time it is or what o'clock
the world starts and stops. You get
to be fifty by walking in the shadow,
playing your music with your eyes
closed tight, walking out the back way
before the last sound has settled

through the saloon. You get to be fifty
by remembering what a nigger slave
your granddaddy smelt like, like all his life
it is a blue smell, like crushed grass,
and the heavy taste of dirt in the skin.

Thieving

When does the debt end? How long must pass
to make up for your hundred years of taking
from people everything they had and giving
nothing in return? When is the debt
full paid? How much thieving and
killing must a man do before it turns
into sin, when all he is doing is taking
back what was taken from him, from
his father, from his father's father?

How many bales of cotton must a man
steal to make up for all the cotton
he picked that went into somebody
else's pocket, somebody else's belly?

How many stacks of wood can you
take before you have covered
all the losses; before you have
repaid what a man has done
to that pink private place
of your mother's mother, that thing
that left her covered in shame
for the rest of her life?

How many pianos can you steal for the
bones in the backwoods, for
the anthem of those leading
us to the blackened bloated bodies
of those boys who they lynched
at midnight under flambeau light,
how much thieving can a body do
before it balances things out?

How much can you take to feed the gap
in a people's memory, the erasure
of the language of the ancestors,
the deafness they caused you
to the whisper of the gods, the house
of bones, the valley of bones,
the deep-rift valley of bones,
covered by the weight of the Atlantic,
where the water stripped these bodies
of all their flesh, all they had
in the bowels of their undoing?

How much does a man have to steal
before he can say, "Now I have
all they took, now all I am getting
is what they got fair and square;
now we are even; now I have
what is mine, and every time
I take from them from now on,
you can call it thieving"?

Elevator

You learn faith in that elevator,
faith and service; learn how to believe,
learn how to make others believe,
learn how to take people where they must go,
where they are scared to go, away from
where they have been; you learn to
be the guide, the prophet, you teach
them the constancy of God, you press
a button, call out a number and it will
climb all the way up; here you learn
how to fly in the house, you reach
into the heavenly places above it all,
and you are Lord of your kingdom,
here where you can pray, so close,
so close, so close to the mountain top.
And it isn't hard to hear the pain
of people, see the bruises in a face,
listen to the lament of those who want
to fly some other way. Since
the market crashed, since Roosevelt
come out like a granddaddy
and tell people to hold on, tell
them how he's got something
for you, you've seen how shiny
a white man's suit can get, how
black his collar, how worn
down the heels of them women
with their stockings painted
to hide the holes, or no
stockings, and you feel like
the angel in the architecture
riding up and down. And you

know that this is why a man
must turn to God, build
a church, know that this is just
the cage where a bird will sing;
for you know how riding this
box to heaven and then down
to hell could teach you what
it feels like for the Holy Ghost
to light your head aflame. And you
know you want your sanctuary
there in the neighborhood, to be a box
taking folks as high as they can go;
know that at least you can say
you own this, you own this, 'cause
you built it with your own two hands.
And all you want to do is let
your people own you, let them
shelter you, so you can give
them the guiding, be the elevator
man running them up to higher
places, to the mountain top.
So just hold on, hallelujah,
just hold on, amen;
just hold on, we going up!

Avery

fling me the stone
that will confound the void
find me the rage
and I will raze the colony
fill me with words
and I will blind your God
                    —Kamau Brathwaite, "Negus"

The plague of messiahs arrives thirty
years into this pathological century;
and the apostate scribes have
turned each crisis of faith into
a punch line. In Trinidad, Man-Man
complains about the fool who pelts
too large a stone while he hangs on
the cross, so we laugh as he, like
Bedward, the wingless flyer, is taken
away, like that Jesus man
on Guyana's wild coast whose
demise is not so funny,
because we knew that these
God men have spoken
an Ital truth shattering the myth
of the auburn-haired Jesus
with his stoic chin and Aryan
eyes. These Garvey men, these Howells,
these John the Baptists, these Averys
have made the hearts of the poor
black folk fill with something
holy: the belief in the comeliness
of black-skinned folks and their hands.

Africa is paradise, and priests
and kings live inside our skins.
It is not so funny when a man
spits on the lies of those missionaries
against our denigration, not so funny
to think of the women sitting
alone in the makeshift chapel
of captured zinc walls and rough-hewn
benches, an altar of boxes and carefully
nurtured plants in cheese pans,
their faces full of questions,
wondering what is next
while their prophets have been
sent to the asylum,
wondering how faith
is kept in the face of such
loss. Not so funny to know
that in 1936, the anointing
of prophecy was upon
ordinary men, or ordinary women,
ordinary black folk, and the world
could not comprehend it—these stones
hurled to confound the void.

The Burden

So sometimes you just want to shoot the poet
because he carries no piano, no guitar,
no horn; the poet is just a head
of conundrums; and you know that
this divining music man, this trickster
with two faces—one to ritualize
holiness, the other to sniff out
the perfume and money in a woman's
skin—this filthy priest with clean
eyes and stained hands is the shadow
you carry for months while these
spirits swirl around you. Young
man, you will die young once
you have exorcised this century
of souls, cast them out into light,
into the bodies of the penitents,
the broken hearts of actors who
give of themselves each night.
Young man, you have always
had an old soul, an ancient
poet's soul, and your back has
carried every instrument of praise
there is—a sack of noises
dragging you down while you
walk through this world. And
sometimes you forget yourself
because this poet consumes you,
and you wonder who is talking,
who is carrying you down, and you
want to shoot the poet; but
this is all you have left,
quick-stepping dance man,

this is all that makes you breathe,
this journeyman of many voices,
who sometimes, after eating
his fill of the world, will stretch
out and sleep, leaving you
light for a spell, easy in your skin,
finding the calm of death.

To Buy a Pair of Shoes

I got shoes
You got shoes
All God's children got shoes . . .
                    —Traditional song

The box, sturdy and assured, the sign
of money, a casket for something
treasured, something of worth. You
remove the cover and there, like
two loaves, the gleaming shoes,
polished leather, taut with newness,
nesting in thin delicate paper.
And you will try them on, one after
the other, like any other man would
in this city, 'cause people can look
at you, look at the angle of your
hat, look at the cut of your suit,
the way it flows down your body,
and then study the shape of your shoes,
how well you care for them,
how strong they plant you down,
and know that no matter how
you came by them, you were good
for the soft shape in the leather,
good for the clean stitches of sole
to skin, good for the money
it would take to walk out of this shop
with these shoes. The thing is,
you are black, you are a true black,
not a simple black, but the deep
black of an Alabama negro;

you are not the color of Booker T,
or Weldon Johnson, or Frederick
Douglas, or Langston Hughes,
or W. E. B. Du Bois—no, no, not
the high-color negro, the kind
that make white folks feel at ease;
no, you are the affront, you are
the stone confounding the void,
you are the stumbling block,
you are that South Carolina
low-country Geechie strain
of negro, with no stain of white
in your skin, with the film
of yellow in your eyeballs.
You are cousin to Jack Johnson,
kin to Marcus Garvey, and sulking
Paul Laurence Dunbar is your
brother—negroes so black
the pure glow off of their skin
is something holy, something
as heroic as a pitch night; and as you
smile with a mouthful of even teeth,
everything about you inviolate,
clean, clean like these shoes,
as you walk out of the store
cradling this box full of grace,
and you imagine all the pavements
you will walk along, all the thick
fine carpets your will glide over,
and all those dust yards you will
pick your way through, all that saw-
dust and beer spill you will step
through, shuffle in, stomp on,
all the boards you will make
squeal, all the beds that will shelter
these shoes, you imagine

how a foot put forward will
announce your presence as dignity
and power, and you will wait
for the quiet of familiar places
to wear these shoes for the first
time. In that moment,
you discard the old
shoes, worn down to your corn-
covered soles, and slip these new
shoes on, tie them leather laces,
and then stand, feeling the press
of your feet into the embracing
skin of the good cured leather,
and, looking down, you watch
the way the seams of your trousers
land lightly and perfectly
on the intersecting lines of the laces,
and you feel the bigness inside you,
for a man is a man with a new
pair of shoes, and you feel to blow
a song so new and fresh it will make
people forget what just came before,
a song that will frighten
all those careless Ethiopians
who have gone astray into
the desert, who have forgotten
their way home; and it will
call them home, call them
to the congregation, call them
to that holy ground where those shoes
are glowing in the Sunday light.

Just Play the Damned Tune

Creole wasn't trying any longer to get Sonny in the water. He was
wishing him Godspeed. Then he stepped back, very slowly, filling
the air with the immense suggestion that Sonny speak for himself.
  —James Baldwin, "Sonny's Blues"

Journeyman, he knows all the tricks,
how to make room inside the crowded
belly of a tune for a surprise to wake
up, to let that stirring inside his head,
giving him ideas he could turn into
a surprise, get ahold of him. He knows
how to make space for the talent;
knows the world has rules. He knows how
to sit back, humble himself, draw
light away from him so the surprise
can happen. Journeyman will read
the contract and the rider, will
step outside and look on the marquee
to see whose name is out there,
and when they come, hours
into the rehearsal, and they start
to sing and play, Journeyman knows
to wait for a sound to break out,
before he settles himself into
the music. The talent might just
be an untalented fool, but if his
name is on the paper, then
journeyman knows to make
this talent sound like music.
He knows how to make a bed
for the horn to blow in,
and this sweet bed of sound

is the bedrock, the unostentatious,
unvarnished truth, and journeyman
knows to just play the piece,
let it be what it is, so the talent
can find a place to shine. Journeyman
will always say the talent hit it
out of the park; journeyman is
going to be lying about this
all the time because journeyman
only cares about the cash in hand.
This is how the ordinary man
takes on the world, quietly,
simply, and journeyman has mastered
how to stand invisibly day and night
so that he can live long. Journeyman
will never know what surprises
he has in him. Journeyman will only
know what is outside himself.

The Dance

At first there is stillness, everything in its rightful place,
the chairs scattered in their own order, the music stands
clothed in tidy scores, the lights low, and the silence
in the place is polite, circumspect, just a shuffle
and scratch, polite as decency. At first there is nothing
to fear, the familiar is all they have and there is comfort
in the familiar—the man likes what is familiar,
he has heard it before, knows its name, got a word
for it: "Lively," he says, which does not sound like
what he means. "Good times," he adds. Folks will
like it, this is normal, no sweat stinging
his armpits, no fretting. Then a drunk black man
stumbles in full of expletives, and the chairs look
chaotic, like an accident already happened.
The black people look down, try to look away;
the white people stare and grin. The black man
claps his big hands as if he has walked into the wrong
room, as if a mistake has been made
and he is not sure what the mistake is. He claps
his hands again and we know someone is expecting
this. This is the taste of shame, or the portent
of shame. This is the chaos of a too-loved father,
a piss-drunk mother, her dress damp in the middle,
and you can smell her before she comes close
enough to touch you; it is the face you know
so well until you are all in this room of chairs
and people like this. He claps a third time,
and they know he wants to dance. Someone
touches a rhythm on strings, looking far
away, hoping that he will collapse before he can
dance. But he stumbles into a dance, a foot
lifted, suspended, a beat, two beats, then

on the half beat it lands, and it is too early
to know he already has the rhythm in his head,
in his body. The taste of shame; their eyes
gaze away, but he continues, lifted knee,
swaying arms, a grin big as Friday night, and that
is when the hips circle, the fingers snap,
and the feet slide, then stomp, slide then stomp,
then slide, and a voice, big as a freight train
storming by your side, yet clean as a bell, shatters
the silence. His eyes are wide open, he catches
eyes, he traps your eyes, till you are caught
in the miracle before you as he chants and sings,
as he smiles, chuckles, groans, and you know
that something impossible like sudden flight
is happening, and in this genius of form and soul,
you are saved—saved from the shower of shame.
The genius of his art transforms the hall into
a cavern gleaming with indescribable light
and everything, in that instant, is decent and in order.

Making a Deal

God, it seems, won't make such a deal,
though it is not always clear why this is.
The devil, though, loiters at railroad tracks
cutting through the abandoned back streets
of southern towns, waiting for a middling
talent to come by. The devil traffics
in souls, but it is an easy sale when
the talent stops to contemplate it. He has
a dollar in his pocket, a thumb length
of whiskey in his flask, and his horn
or guitar or harmonica or fiddle is all
he has that he can put a price on. His
soul is mostly a word somebody told him
about in church or in the Gospel
Home, where the soup was a little
salty and thin but always hot, and the bread
was freshly baked and sweet. But he
has never seen his soul, never touched
it, never smelt it, never tasted it, even
though, they say, it is somewhere inside
him. He has yet to reason that it was never
his to buy or sell in the first place,
anyway, and he can't tell for sure
if he has one. Now, his dick he can
look at; it grows and shrinks, it fills
his hand, it winks at him, it breathes,
and a lot of women say they can feel it
when it presses in. Cut that off,
and a man has lost something he knows
he used to have—a piece of him is gone.
But the soul, well, it is like this thing
in him that makes him know when

a sound he makes is right, how he can
feel better than the next person, how
people say, "You got it" like "it" can be
bought or sold, held up, rubbed up against.
So when the devil, picking his teeth
in the hot sun, boots shining like a new
penny, looks the man in the eye and says,
"Give me your soul and I will give you
talent, more talent than you know what
to do with," well, somebody has to be pulling
a fast one, somebody's getting a better
deal than somebody else—somebody is
a sucker and somebody isn't. The man
knows that if he can deal with the devil
like this, then he is going to hell anyway,
so all he's got is now, and now is big
as the sky, and now is the world of good
times and power. Florsheim shoes and
a tailored suit. The deal is easy: nothing
for nothing and the music is sweet over
the dry-backed southern town.

News from Harlem

Seven miles of Black Star Liners coming in the harbour . . .
—Fred Locks, 1975

For Marcus Mosiah Garvey Jr.

Even here on the south side of this city
of wind and blood, news is good for negroes.
A fat-faced, true African man, one of
those black men you know never
had a doubt that he is a man and strong;
one of those magic men
who know what God must feel like
standing over an army of angels; one
of those men who's stood at the edge
of the new century and seen a wide
world of what could be; a man who,
when he heard what Du Bois said
about the color line, thought right off
that this is going to be a century
where everybody will be talking
about niggers like they are new money
and he, sure as hell, is going
to shine and shine. A man
with two big hands and a head
full of words who knows the freedom
of nothing to lose; a man who
knows the long legacy of rebels,
those maroons whispering Akan
in the hills—knife men, cutlass men,
roots men, Congo men,
those yellow-eyed quiet men
who look at death like it is

a good idea that someone came up
with; a man who learned by
touching the split chest of a white
man, his heart still thumping,
everything inside him slick
with blood and water, his ribs
pulled aside where the doctor
tried, that white men
ain't nothing but flesh, old rotting
flesh like everybody else;
a man who's done the math
and knows that for fifty years
his people have been waiting
for something bigger than themselves.
Well, news has it that this man
is causing trouble in Harlem
and the world won't be the same
when he's done with it. Even
here, the excitement of it is
rushing through the blues joints
and people are strutting about like
they have been marching, like
they been waving flags, like *they* shouting
the name of freedom beside
the round-faced black man,
with his proud high voice
showering imperatives on the folks
who gather to hear him talk
with his sweet island singing.
Black man sweating, dressed
clean with high collar and good
shoes. Yeah, this is good news
walking, cause we all need a daddy,
a man with a good firm voice,
a man who knows what we must
do to change this wearying world,

a man with a head full of dreams
of ships, seven miles of them
coming into that gaping Hudson
mouth, red, gold and green flags
flapping in the air—seven miles
of ships as far as the eye can see,
coming in, coming, in coming in.

Initiate

Cutting across the stretch of cotton trees
to switch back where the stand of live oaks
gives shade for the sharecroppers, where
lunch is a single black pot of yams,
ham hocks, okra and a slippery density
of greens; under there, you can push
through the old forest and find yourself
where the best moonshine is stilled.
Most days, everything is quiet—the air
smelling of salt and jasmine—except
for the twang of a guitar darting
through the trees like the loneliest
sound in the world. And a gravel-
rough voice, full of the sweetness
of warm damp flesh and the satisfaction
of a long gulp of pure factory-made
bourbon—the way it spreads across
the chest, the familiar swirl of pleasure
in the head when the world
brightens for an instant; that sound
of a man and his guitar, and the thump
of heels on the board, make
me stand still as a ghost, right
there behind the old shack,
and the way my belly feels is like
a lie I have been caught in
or the shudder in my body
when the press of a river rush
beats off the rock against
my groin; this voice is like sin
on me, that feeling of tender need
and the lasting tingle of the after.

He is singing about a woman,
about a train, about that jug,
and I know without nobody telling
that if this song was a piece
of clothing, it would be my panties
and my stockings, it would be
the ribbon, red as a tease, in my hair;
it would be a scarf whipping
against my face. This is how
love had a language for me,
how I learned the niceness
of longing, the full-bellied weight
of need, the blues of desire;
this is how I learned to make
circles with my waist, and feel
the wind teasing my skin to a tingle.
And when the song ends,
I cry for the lonesome
sky wide above me, for the absence
of all the sound in the world.

The Lost Tribe

1
Stones

I have arrived at the edge of the barrier islands
and beyond this is the pidgin of a dark sea.
Even the foam has a brown tint; the grand
waves rise and fall restless as these dreams
I have had, curled on the straw and packed
mud of my bed. I have arrived here and looked
out beyond the entanglement of these stacked-
up grasses and bramble and the fierce hooks
of thorns, followed the scent of the water
as if somehow I could find home when
the beach is still pocked with the slavers'
paraphernalia—a busted pirogue, black coffles,
rotting cotton clothes mummifying the bare bones
of dead slaves—but all I find are silent stones.

2
The Language of Birds

After three hundred years she imagined she would
know the language of birds. Yet each dawn,
walking through the slick dew-heavy woods,
she can't read the scattered calls. She frowns
at her alienness; not yet, she can't call this home.
The fruits are too firm—she is used to the soft
fleshiness of mangoes and pawpaws. She comes
here to find the leaves and seeds she stuffs
into her blackened leather pouch that smells
of the densest shadows of a forest's womb.

The path back is towards light, the swell
of quarreling spirits at her back. The bloom
of a sun breaking open is the one familiar
dialect she knows—the promise of fire.

3
Memory

Now in the city, she has not stepped out
of the gloom of her home for thirty years.
Now she lives on the memory of boats
bobbing on the unsettled water, the clear
air of a mountain walk, the feel of wind
on the skin. It is all memory now, and she
has not walked the gravel path to the plots
where the dead are buried. "Let all these
dead people bury themselves," she coughs,
and announces the shelter of walls
as a final birthright. She has brought
the forest into this solid musky hovel
where vines crawl along the walls and the air
is thick with potions and healing tears.

4
Arrival

Here is the simple truth: I was told how
those useless barren islands came to be
crowded with the mutterings and low
moanings of thousands; they are lost beyond the sea,
the story goes, bumping into each other,
meeting in confused circles, making and unmaking
laws. They are blind to each gesture
by the chiefs who have also forgotten

the language of return. They will stumble
around, singing laments into the yellowing
leaves, until they find someone who knows the temple
of bones beneath the sea, the calming
of the bone mansions, the resting place
of the dead, the kingdom of constant grace.

The Host of Holy Witnesses

1
For Frederick Douglass

To think right there is where Booth stood, a squat
negro in a suit is talking about the rights
of white folk and the law that they've got
tied up with their rights; imagine tonight,
a stage full of ordinary black people
looking like my slavey family, turning
our heads aflame over a piano's simple
music, and I can tell the spirits rising
are old as dirt, old as my skin, and my heart
swells to know that these white folks
will see how we have come so far,
how we can call on ghosts to choke
the beasts that held us back so long,
Lord, we come through so bold, so strong!

2
For Harriet Tubman

August, you are red like some white man's
bastard, like one of those negroes who would
never leave with me because your chance
for a good life was best where you stood;
but, Lord, you know yourself, and how you know
the voice of those spirits that used to talk
to me, tell me where to turn, tell me where to go;
how you know the heart of a people locked
down in that slave century, how you know
the songs to sing like that? My heart

feels lighter now, tells me that we showed
you something and you doing your part
like we all did; and we still here
still standing, still holding on right here.

3
For Jack Johnson (Better?)

Forgive me for not moving beyond the well
where they must have found him by the stench
of his body or the flies' cacophonic spell
of alarm—how they found the sour bitch wedged
between the mossy walls, his neck broken,
his busted head black with dried blood;
when they came, a blanket of flies rising
sluggishly to fill the sky. He did not know God,
did not know what breeze off the tracks
could remember all his sins, the brothers
he slaughtered, the women he smacked
about before taking his sick pleasures.
Forgive me for the sweet hum in my throat.
We who captained the boat will go down with the boat.

4
For W. E. B. Du Bois

> If I got one thing against the black chappies, it's this—no one gives
> it to you. You have to take it.
> —Frank Costello, in *The Departed,* directed by
>   Martin Scorsese

He puts the question well: Tradition
or progress? The spirits in the piano
sold for a plot of land, a piece of a nation

so intent on burying us with sorrows,
sell the bloodied past for the hope
of a tomorrow, as if memory and spirit
can be lost, as if we could all cope
with the absence of history. He tells it
well, the conundrum, but is soft
on the answers. Still a sweet entertainment,
this crowding of the poor and bereft;
so much is said in a laborer's pronouncement.
But it is not enough for a future,
if we are to thrive and endure.

5
For Paul Laurence Dunbar

The preacher man counts his coins each day.
In the city you can pretend a heroic past—
a high-ranking soldier slaughtering the grey-
coated confederates, a patriotic cast
of relatives and friends—you can invent
dreams, riding up and down the elevator,
ferrying white folks who sometimes vent
about stocks and the changing weather,
like you know something, and if you're lucky
they will let you say a poem or two;
a way to make a living to beat back memory
that will snare your feet, consume you.
I like the preacher, I know him well,
caged bird riding between heaven and hell.

6
For Zora Neale Hurston

Thank God they letting you sing and dance,
talk your vernacular, spin your potions,

and the women take and throw to chance
the men they want and speak what notion
come to their head. Thank the Lord
the negro can be a negro, all alone
on the stage. Welcome, welcome aboard,
I have been waiting for so long,
and now everybody's doing it. Maybe
I feel a little cheated, but I've had
my little spell with glory,
so I will settle myself and not say a bad
word about how ordinary our heroes are
or how to get here we must have traveled far.

PART THREE

Reading the Sky

Talk

No one quarrels here, no one has learned
the yell of discontent—instead, here in Sumter,
we learn to grow silent, build a stone
of resolve, learn to nod, learn to close
in the flame of shame and anger
in our hearts, learn to petrify it so;
but the more we quiet our ire,
the heavier the stone. This alchemy
makes concrete in the vein, and even
the sludge of affront will calcify
until the heart, at last, will stop,
unassailable, unmovable, adamant.

Find me a man who will stand
on a blasted hill and shout,
find me a woman who will break
into shouts, who will let loose
a river of lament, find the howl
of the spirit; teach us the tongues
of the angry so that our blood—
my pulse—our hearts flow
with the warm healing of anger.

You, August, have carried in your belly
every song of affront your characters
have spoken, and maybe you waited
too long to howl against the night,
but each evening, on some wooden
stage, these men and women
learn to sing songs lost for centuries,
learn the healing of talk, the calming
of quarrel, the music of contention,
and in this cacophonous chorus,
we find the ritual of living.

Penitentiary

On another stretch of your journey, say along the Mississippi River
Delta, you see rows and rows of black prisoners chained together
working in fields under the careful vigil of armed overseers. At first
you wonder, has slavery really been abolished in the South? But
your guide assures you that these are *convicts* on the chain gang,
not slaves.

> —Mark Colvin, *Penitentiaries, Reformatories,
> and Chain Gangs*

Workhouse,
Crab louse
Life is worth much more than gold . . .
We apply but dem turn down parole
Conviction,
Emancipation
Freedom is a must
In Jah almighty do I put my trust.

> —Gregory Isaacs, *"Idren Gone a Jail"*

It is the hut in the wilderness among the bramble
and acacia bushes, the flat-headed boabab, stingy
with its shade; it is the haunt of dust-covered mangy
creatures, the stench of tooth and claw; it is the path
of stone and thorns, the shame-old-lady, a dull
green shrub closing its leaves to the touch of a foot
misplaced; it is the alertness and caution of prickles
and hardened earth; it is the sun relentless in the sky,
the freemasonry of water finders, the secrets
of rainmakers; it is the boney shoulders of pot-
bellied babies, scratching their arms, staring at you,
their skins white with caked mud, their knowing
seeing; it is the way the sun sets red over the land,

the lines of red dirt climbing towards the clouds;
it is the slow shuffle of a coffle of men, in single
file, their heads shaved to a gleam, their eyes
red with the daze of chewed leaves, their arms
swinging, bodies bare in the setting sun—
men, still boys, who coming so far out in the wilderness
are nervous at the growl of creatures in the shadow;
it is the place where their foreskins will be shed,
where they will learn the efficiency of knives,
where blood will be spilled and sipped
to the shattering of screams, where they will see
the dark lines of the griots, arms waving against the fire,
where they will know nothing and everything, where
they will learn the names of their brothers,
the warm voices of their brothers, the lament
of their brothers, the lament of their brothers;
it is here in this barren place where all music
comes as a croak at first then tastes like God
in the wind; it is like this, like this, this ritual
march into the belly of the beast, and we know
that only some return whole, only some return
at all; that only some imagine this as other than
it should be. Our men are in search of the primordial
rituals of maturation, and find it in the bastardized
edifices of their undoing, of this Parchman.

Art

The streets that Balboa walked were his own private ocean, and
Balboa was drowning.
> —Entire text of "The Best Blues Singer in the World,"
> a short story by August Wilson

You know when to stop, how to set limits;
counting the days, your body is your art
and when your art was done, so were you.
Here I am now, taking your economy,
multiplying it, foolishly—perhaps, but
who wants to be the wicked servant,
derided by the master for being mean,
for playing for par, for toeing the line,
for holding steady, for hanging in there?
You were no hard taskmaster, you give us
the skeletons from the graveyard
of your private ocean, and I will
build this mansion of bones, this
edifice of polished bones glinting
in the sun. Oh, this art and the waves
rising; you go forth like a blues-
man looking for dry ground for swimming
out into the dark water; you push
forward, feeling for the security
of shifting sand until nothing holds
you but the eddy of the water,
and you hold your head up, breathe,
trying to learn the rhythm of the waves
so your nose will not fill with salt
burning, so you will not be covered,
your pate like an islet at high tide.

Every song is an adventure into the gloom,
as if you know that by kicking
against everything, you will find
comfort, the music of arrival.
Ma Rainey sings into the dark; her blues
is the sound of a soul finding
breath in the swirl of waves; this
is the way metaphors will save us.
August came without announcement,
and the air thickened to the sluggish
pace of last breaths of an asthmatic. I'm tired
these days; my children's laughter
is the lingering light before the night.
Here is the path of my own art,
the way I soften with my wife's
thigh pressing on my knee; the waves
lift me, a clumsy dream overtakes me,
confusing me when I awake.

Mother, the Great Stone Got to Roll

White cruciform—a crossing of planks
on a sturdy pedestal planted three feet
into the earth—like a still propeller,
the blades are bright against the green
of croton bushes; a mango tree overhangs
and the sudden alarm of hibiscus
tree bursts with bloom. On each
corner of the planks is balanced
the clean glow of rum bottles
cut through by sunlight through trees,
the labels scrubbed away—bottles
filled with water, holy as fresh
first rain. An enamel bowl sits
at the center of the circle; a vessel
for a fist of white candles, embossed
thick veins entangling the solid
phalanx. Here you will find the evidence
of spirits if you look carefully;
the tiny feathers of caged doves
stirring in the cool air, the hum
of voices like wings startled
and then finding the calm of
evening. An old woman stands
at the door, old enough to know
a thought before it leaves the mouth
of a stranger; old enough to let it
come out, flutter in the air,
settle itself in the dark
room, before she offers hope
or a quiet curse of prophecy.
This woman is
the lighter of candles, the mutterer

of tongues, the keeper of dreams,
the interpreter of tragedies,
the rememberer of the dead,
the music of the living,
the sermon rising over the world.
She holds in her palm
the coil of dog shit which she sniffs,
reads carefully. She is never
frightened by death. The door
is always ajar; she reminds us:
"This is a peaceful house."

The Drowning

Like a quick impulsive plunge
for cool after the hot of liquor;
after the filth of sex with the woman
leaning over the open window,
trying to be casual as ritual;

from far a man sprints up
the incline of the bridge, a speck
of brown on the bone white
of the dried-out road. He waits
for a horse to pass, then leaps.

The crowd gathers at the jetty;
he is far enough out for waves
from the tugboats with gleaming
beams of steel piled up to cover
and uncover his bobbing head.

It is strong enough, this black
swirl, to pull him downstream
under the bridge towards the bank
crowded with rotting crates, where
the constable stands shouting.

He will not come any closer, lights
out to the deep with quick
strokes. The crowd points, shouts.
The constable pulls out his gun.
The man's head rises up, then sinks.

They will find his body among
the rocks, his loose trousers tangled

among the sharp edge of stone,
his eyes closed tight. A woman
laments. Most people look down.

He leapt as if he had to swim
to the far end of the river, as if
the thought of a ferry or a long
walk around the city was too much.
He is gone as quickly as he plunged.

A Name

For "Black" Mary Wilkes

When you worship at my altar,
you will find the black sleeve of my
tender skin cradled in the unfolded
lips of people; you will see how soft
black can be, how full, how you can
adore the way wet gleams to light
when black is damp and tender.
There you will know beyond
all knowing that what pulls you
is as irrevocable as birth, that what
keeps you transfixed and uncertain
is the silence of this noise, is
the sleeping mouth offering up
speeches that no one else will
hear but you. Lord, this door-
way to impossible journeys
can fill you with dread. You
will feel about it what you
feel about home, the comforts,
the pull of the familiar, and every
scent that triggers tears,
deep melancholy and the wild
abandon of childish laughter;
in the face of this altar you can't
lie without shame; you can't
walk away unchanged. You will
want to cradle it, gaze at its
simple grace, slap it, bruise it,

push away from it, place your
mouth upon it and drink; you
will want to tell it secrets,
whisper confessions, and then
take deep breaths so you won't
forget the scent of your beginning,
the scent of your end. In this
place, this root-nurturing soil,
this graveyard to all strength,
you will ask her her name,
knowing, at last, that she does
have a name, and she will say,
"Black Mary, that's my name."

The White Man's Burden

Wilmington, North Carolina, 1898

Waddle stands at the doorway frowning,
belly of a patrician, jaw set firm; he knows
that this sturdy edifice will be burning
in minutes—negro property, the grand show
of their progress—that of Alexander Manly,
bastard child of some backroom screw—
a white man planting seed with impunity
and joy, to make a litter of uppity stock,
fools like this nigger—who thinks he is
somebody. This printing press, this *Record,*
will burn, and folks will know who is
in charge, simple as that. It is hard
to wreck a beautiful building, but right
is right and this is the burden of being white.

Black Suits

Wilmington, North Carolina, 1898

From the top of this street I can see
the slow procession of black-suited men,
black men, proud-headed, now bowed trees,
their feet kicking up dust—five, ten,
fifteen—all our dignity in scraggly single
file, heading towards the station; they will
board the train, a phalanx of whites wrangling
for a chance to spit at them. The dead chill
of fall hangs over everything. From here
we watch the shame of our brokenness,
the usurpation of all we have gained
since the bedlam of that war's madness.
A coup, an insurrection, the white stain
of white supremacy. Our men must leave;
tomorrow we follow, now begins our grief.

Postbellum

They never used to hate us like this,
this hate that sits on their skin
like a plague, covers their necks
with rashes, makes them spit every
time they look at us, every time
our eyes meet; a sick kind of pallor
on their skins, the look of people
so close to death they've already
seen the shadow looming; never
used to look like they could kill
for killing's sake, the way they walk
like broken branches after
a hurricane has crashed through
the forest; sharp edges, clumsy
limbs, heads bowed; and when
they look, there is nothing but
cold in their eyes. Not even when
a nigger stole some food, or raised
a hand to a white man, not
when they crowded a running
buck, his head full of Canada,
his mouth full of "Kill me now!"
Not when Miss Odom dragged
me into the parlor, told me to
lift my frock so she could
lay that switch on me so
I could bleed to remember
not to cut my eye anywhere near
her; even then, she gave me a warm
wet rag, and whispered soft
as cotton, "It will burn for a few days
but it will heal," as if somewhere

love wanted to come out. But not
now. The guns are silent now.
Soldiers look like hobos walking
through the dust, jittery eyes trying
to run from something they can't
stop seeing; and they hate us
like God hates sin; hate how we
smell, hate how we talk, hate
how we sing. You can't tell
with them no more. They say, "Y'all
is free," like they announcing our
death. They say we can't leave
the district, can't leave this
town; can't jump on a train,
can't go nowhere. But they say.
"Y'all is free!" and laugh. This
country smell of death. Walk in
the forest and you bound to find
a bloated body of some poor
nigger who opened his mouth
every mile you walk. The flies
so drunk they don't move for nobody.

Alabama, 1898

They come early and we supposed to wait
right there under the big pecan tree
so they can take us with them to the fields;
then we must work there until noon time.
They feed us grits and a piece of smoked ham
hocks and a long drink of river water;
and then we go back out when the cold
is blowing off the river; and we work
till the sweat dries on our face to salt.
We walk back slow, some of us singing,
some of us looking at the train pushing
through those cotton fields heading north
and nobody wants to say what is in
their hearts; that it is like they put
an angel of fire with a long sword
and then saying, "These niggers going to
stay right here in Paradise for as long
as cotton's got to be picked, as long
as tobacco got to be gathered; as long
as clothes need washing; as long as
babies need raising; these niggers
won't be going nowhere." That is what
the angel says standing on the high-
way; that is what the angel saying
when he stands in front of the train
station; he won't take our money;
he says it isn't enough even though
the sign says exactly what you have
in your hand. Jim Crow and his cousin
keep singing and plucking that banjo;
and they saying that they love their
negroes, love to keep them home, don't

want any of them taking the highway
to feed the factories of those Northerners.
So we reach home, and these days
old folks whispering it's all the same,
just like the old days, just like bondage,
only we ain't worth shit to these
crackers no more, ain't no price
on our head; we are cheap as dirt;
they can break our bones and nobody
going to lose a thing. We are just
bodies, free to be battered, free to be
used; and they hate every laughter
we can give; hate the way we
walk. Old people starting to call this
freedom a curse, say better we
were back when nobody dreamed
of freedom. We need Sister Moses
to come back with her song, we
need a man to resume the living;
but for now, we sleep, quiet-quiet,
waiting for the trumpet to sound.

Seventeen

After a while the locks grow overworn with use,
the screws get loose, and the gate flaps,
careless; the water flows, quick as change
filling up the low bank gutter until the overspill
spreads into the valley, turning slopes
into heavy swamp; the gaping gate—
no gardening here; the wood is fat with
water swell—this is the dream she has
for ten nights: a flooded plain, a house
floating on a lake crowded with debris,
the remains of a sudden storm,
bats, trousers, a piano with a gaping
hole, a guitar covered in moss, an upright ornate
armchair, a listing wooden trunk
moving with dignity, nudging the flapping
gate before sliding in; an instrument
probing the loose thighs of a woman
who has learned not to argue with
prophecy but to praise the prophet
loud enough to distract him—perhaps
to drown his words. The mountains—
oh the mountains—on Mount Zion
our prophets gathered to seek God's
face. Seventeen rings; seventeen men
have stayed long enough to believe
in the ownership of property, long
enough to stake claim—never uncertain
of their right to this woman with a mouth
so tender and ripe it can distract even
the surest man from his journey. Seventeen
rings; they have come to Aunt Ester
in a dream, a way to understand how

this world will teach a woman to gather
to herself the things she has never had.
Seventeen rings; seventeen men come
to plant their seed only to find a river
of bloated corpses; the sluggish twist
and turn of bodies floating downriver
after a storm. Eventually a man will wake
and see in this dark skin, this impossibly
beautiful skin, the haunting of shipwrecks
in storms, the decay of barren soil,
the remnants of catastrophes in her vagina;
that fruit that can hold them
and drag from them everything they have
cherished. Seventeen rings, a simple
revelation. She smiles, declares she has
stopped counting now. It is hard
not to believe her, yet harder to trust her tongue.

The Old Woman on the Road

Hard not to want somebody standing by
the road with a bucket of water, somebody
ordinary but with eyes old as anything
around you to tell you that it is alright.
Who wouldn't want to hear a woman
singing a baby song, a lullaby at the edge
of the night, something to calm you,
make you sleep because you know
that when you wake she will be
there, her hands smelling of thyme,
garlic and onions; her rheumy
eyes still alive with questions
and knowing, her spotted skin basic as dirt,
and her gravel voice—such a calming thing
for you. Yes. You can't blame me
for searching out the woman on
the hill, the woman with a bandana,
and a long skirt stained with the dew
and grass from the thick bushes;
a woman with arms taut as
a tree's limbs, a woman who will
hear all your sins and tell you
that you will still live until
tomorrow, a woman who will
embrace your body wracked
with disease and let you know
that crossing the water is not as harsh
as you might have thought,
to tell you that there is more light
in the grave than you may think.
We are all looking for the woman
with two hundred years under

her skin, the woman who can
touch you and remind you
that there are things bigger
than the sky, bigger than today.
And what we fear most is that
we will travel for years
always looking for her, but
never find her. We fear
this more than our nightmares.

Shod

the soil
Is bare now, nor can foot feel, being shod.
—Gerard Manley Hopkins, "God's Grandeur"

Once, I walked for miles with shoes,
stepped into a pumpkin field and felt
the embrace of soil. A nest of chiggers
would grow between my toes for weeks
before I knew to dig them out. But on
that pumpkin patch, the rush of light
rising up my legs was too much.
They arrived like a storm, those voices,
up my legs, through my hips, taking me.
Could not move, had to hold my body
straight, had to let it sway when they said
I should sway, had to bend, had to holler
words I did not know. That and them
chiggers was it for me. Sometimes, though,
I long to walk out, naked feet and all,
into the soil of a freshly plowed field
with lumps of steaming clay probed
by the gleaming of worms; I long to stand
there and listen for the train to come rushing in.

Rope

To hold our lives together on the cart
before the slow march after midnight
along back roads, blind-driving, the scent
of the exhaust making us drowsy, every
shadow in the fields a threat of sorts,
we use rope thick as two thumbs side by side,
pulling hard on the knot to keep our
parts from falling by the wayside. We
have kept this rope supple with oil,
constant use, never letting it stay
idle long enough to rot. It is hard
to look at the coiled silence of our
strongest rope and not think of what
it has held: the heavy grey-green
battered bucket knocking the stone
sides of the wall, top water spilling
back down, this cherished substance,
carrying our lives; the mare, white
and grey, plodding across the wide
open field at dusk, her head heavy
with labor, the rope a caress
against her neck, the way she
turned towards a gentle tug. We
hold the balance of our need
in this rope. The dead weight
of Junebug at dawn, his skin still
steaming, his beautiful black skin
catching the morning light, tender
among the leaves; we found him
there, his neck stretched, the wrapping
of several yards of taut rope
around the drooping branch.

We undid the knot, let his body down
into our arms, then carried the rope
like a soldier's flag behind the shaking cart
as it bore his swollen body.
This ordinary rope, this gift
we cannot forget, this remembrance
of what we have lost. Someday
a soul will come out of the fields
to claim it, and then we will know.

Thief

After Caesar Barlow

> T'ief from t'ief, God laugh.
> —Jamaican proverb

A grown man, even a boy, standing on the corner
laughing or looking, his empty hands dangling,
that is a thief. Pick him up, lock him up.

A thief still has shame; doesn't want a soul
to know he is a thief. Can't look you in the eye.
A thief is worse than a murderer—he has shame.

Nobody will thief from you with blood
in his head. No, a thief will walk by you,
smile with you for a whole week, and then strike.

Give a thief money, he won't know what
to do. Put a quarter on the table, walk
away, a thief will know what to do.

You can't fix a thief. It is in the blood.
A thief will look on your body and say
he wants what it can do. He will hire you.

A thief can see a woman's soul, know
her spirit, know how to talk to it. He will
make her cry out, take that sound and run.

When a thief is done with you, he look
like God—the way he comes when you don't
know, the way he makes you pray for peace.

But laugh with an open mouth in front of a thief,
he will steal your breath, leave you with
five years less in your future, leave you bereft.

A thief comes by where there is plenty. He
will stand around and watch your song floating
from your throat. Next thing, he makes a record.

When a man comes to you with a box, to
say he wants to take your picture, you got
to know that every time he does, you fade a little.

Only one thing to do with a thief. Hound him,
call the world on him, let everyone get
a piece of him; let the dog lick his blood.

An Unfinished Life

He said he had heard that the cold up North
kept a body fresh like ice days in South Carolina's
winter will keep butchered flesh fresh for weeks.
He heard say that up there in Pittsburgh a black
man's innards could last much longer; first
the cold and then a dose of brown liquor to pickle
the softer parts make them last. Garret Brown
got that clean black-as-coal look that only
Gullah folk from Summerville got, the kind
you see in white shirt, skinny boy with a
round-as-a-penny face running errands here
and there; that was a boy turning into a man—
slavery still carrying its old stench in the air.
1873, they started walking 'cause everybody
told his mother that Charleston is an auction
block. "Charleston is too hot for negroes,
Charleston will break a black man with
fear." This is why Garret Brown started
walking—first to Louisville, Kentucky,
then as a man with a head full of
dreams, over the hills and valleys,
across the rivers and streams, into
the metal sky of Pittsburgh where the green
is cool as the air, and everything
lasts forever. Well, Mr. Garret Brown
is dead; his lungs rotted out, and the cold
just stopped up everything in him,
made his bones shake with fever
each day. Yes, cold will preserve
everything, good and bad, like all that sad
feelings he would feel when he heard news
of the deaths in his family down there on

those sea islands where the body worked
itself to death to fatten those white folks
summering in Greenville, while the muggy
rice fields cooked the souls of black folk,
making a short life a blessing down there,
while he coughed away his unfinished
living in this cold place. So we stay
silent, take a breath for Garret Brown,
dead in the height of his power, dead
at 44; gone, gone; and the swirl of snow
in the air holds us still in our
perpetual sorrow; fresh as the scent
of newly butchered meat on ice.

Migrant

Together at last, our company stops for water
under a live oak tree, its muscular branches stretching
over the body, a cooling place. Two men carry
a pail of water pulled from the brook over
the gentle slope where the cows are dotting
the green. Quenched, our dusty faces cleaned
of grit and salt, we stand waiting for the cool
of evening before the next leg of our journey;
another procession in search of an open
field or a cluster of trees with no fence
where we could boil the yams, smoked pork
and fresh tomatoes we harvested from the Crawford
farm after the shedding of hog blood into the soil,
the comfort of the breaking of bread and prayer.
There in the gloom a flat voice will rise
around the fire, a voice so basic it longs
for the company of the humble. The voices
arrive, at first breaking slowly from bodies
now wounded by weeks of rain, sun,
and the jolt of feet pushing into flattened
roads. They sing, "Guide me, oh, Thou
great Jehovah," the melody of Europe
with its rises, its setting flattened to
a plaintive wail of long belly song,
the harmony washing the pecan leaves
like wind. Everything on our skins stirs
as if God himself is blowing over the sweat,
drying it, easing the fever from killing.
This is how the company will sing,
unhurried, filling the pitch-black night
with the company of ancestors and angels.
In this instant all time will return to itself,

the night will be as true as it has been
for centuries and the air will spark
with the whisper of spirits, a crowd
of holy witnesses whispering, reminding
us of the peace that comes with rest
and the strength we will need to go on,
to find that river, that crossing place,
the Holy Spirit like a cloud above us.
After the water, we walk again. Soon
the shelter of night and the music
of communion. In Alabama, the charred
remains of the church have cooled;
crows peck at the charcoal and ash.
The silence swallows the ruins. We are
heading north, where we will arrive
with the light and with songs on our lips.

Cemetery

So many corpses live in my head.
I am the dumb graveyard of lives
wasted in the pursuit of emptiness.
These are even lanes of good-behaving
bodies in this dull stretch of fields.
There is no mourning in the cemetery
of their unmaking. I carry them, though,
like I do old wounds—the broken eye
that offers a blur making me king
among the blind; the splintered knee-
cap, my praying discipline, teaching
me the penance of pain at the throne
of grace. A fool did that. He too lies
still in the graveyard of my soul;
a dark cloudiness over my pulsing
heart, a bruised fleshiness my
mother's tongue always found as
she stewed me in the lard of my
father's sins. She too must lie
dumb as memory among these
stones. Here I patrol the clean
avenues searching for loiterers. Here
I herd the idly dead: the boy constantly
sprinting in circles with a hole
in the back of his skull, the boy
carrying a loaf of magic bread
stolen from my future. Here in the
boneyard of memory, the law
is my solace, the ordering of things.
I rule all remorse and manage the canker
of regret. I know something about
talking with ghosts. They have no news,

really, they are as daft as they were
walking this earth, and there it is dark,
and they learn nothing new—they live
in loving remembrance; they come over
the river to gossip only, but long mostly
for the taste of living and for surprise.
From this house that I have built
with the pragmatism of an opportunist,
the world seems as uncomplicated
as the hush of wind in my grave-
yard. My sister has left my shelter
for the home of a woman who
communes with the dead. They
indulge in orgies of lamentation
deep into the night before returning
drunk to the orderliness of my
graveyard. I miss my sister
and the comfort of her acceptance,
but it is the price one must pay
for ordering the dead. It is a cold
hard business, this commerce
of silence and stone.

Exile: Reading the Sky

A dollop of white smeared liberally on the off-
white embossed sheet, generous water so the spread
is untidy, the paper pulping, then a tab of blue,
its veins crawling across the uneven surface;
summer before sunlight, then the storm
of black deep in the belly of the white
paste; and the inky morning light over
the steep steel surfaces of the city is Pittsburgh
washed in a constant thin rainfall;
and a shattering crowd of starlings sprints
madly over the gloom like a wild spotted
silk scarf, its carefully embroidered filigree
of leaves swirling over the sorrow
of our mourning. This is how far
from home we are; far from the useless
combustible abundance of pine needles
in a forest, from the red dirt's
annoying stains, from the steaming peach groves,
from the skies that stretch beyond us
towards the sea—a mountain of swollen
clouds filling us with a sense of God
in the heavens. In this city, men no longer
look to the sky for news; we are all
illiterate to this dialect. Rain and snow
always surprise us, and we know that
the crazy birds are drunk with berries
and will die for want of a landing. In this
city those who keep staring south, waiting
for news that the rivers have all fallen
into their walls, and that the land is still
waiting for us to plant seed and trim

the hostas now entangled with dry leaves
over our people's graves, will be disappointed.
More are coming, walking across the bridge,
undone, with nothing but sorrow in their eyes
and a mouthful of questions for ways
to survive in this cold. There are days,
you promise, on a Friday night, with change
hot in your pocket and your stomach
warm with good juice, when you can
catch in the sky a hint of red and the flirtatious
lavender of wisteria . Then you feel
to sing like good old country folk do.

Called

This pure river water, warmed in an enamel
pan, I cup and drip over her feet, letting the dry
callus gleam with color again, softening.

How small your feet are in my hands,
how light a burden, how fine these bones,
how tough your yellow soles.

I rub with thumb, trying to reach back
into every muscle and tendon that has
flexed, heel and toe, how far you've walked.

300 years on these roads—no thorn
can pierce, no sharp stone wound; I have
taken bush trails, slippery river tracks,

steep mountain paths and the hot
pavement of open roads to touch you,
to learn how to pray healing through

my hands. This ritual of pumice stone
scraping white dust off calcified flesh
into the water is how you taught me

to love. And over my head, your
words spill thick and warm, the shine
of prophecy, the oil of calling.

Your fingers find my soft scalp beneath
the chaos of my unruly hair, and your
prayer is like flame over me. Bless me.

You say your memory is long as days;
I say I cannot remember even now
what you said about making cornbread,

or how to heal the green-shit
ailments of infants; or when to steep
fever grass; where the moon should be.

"If you take it, take your calling,
you will have centuries to learn
how to wash a sufferer's feet."

You say this as I cover my palms
with balming grease and smear
your feet to shine and soften;

the menthol makes you sigh,
your fingers squeezing my head,
the anointing heavy over me.

Mist

I am a graveyard.
Here, there is no mourning;
the dead are dumb as wood.

I have forgotten how to cry
because I can see spirits,
as if the graves have broken

open on that red
resurrection morning.
The earth is a mansion

with many floors,
the layering of centuries,
the spirits strolling;

no one crosses the plain;
so many millions
gone, only to return

as if there are many
earths transparent
as the glassy film

of ice over a pond.
I don't know names
anymore; the spirits

(what we call them)
are soft as clouds
or mist, they travel.

These days, I stand
before a boiling pot
until it dries and cracks,

all the steam
caressing me like the love
of the dead. Healing

comes from the spray
of iron on damp cloth,
healing is the scent

of burning, the faltering
of crushed cloth,
the sweat of labor.

I am a graveyard,
wet with sea fog,
my memories

will not let me go.
I am staring upwards
looking for blue

sky through
the crowd of souls
clogging the heavens.

It Begins with the Hog

For Tarleton Blackwell

It begins with pigs; flat, sloppy pigs thickening
his dreams; pink, pudgy pigs in waistcoats.
The painter who works large canvases
smells the bacterial bacchanal of the hog
farm cutting through the air. In the fall
there is the mercy of cleansing chill,
the occasional freeze that lets an artist
dream of cleaner things. But it begins
with pigs—the boar's head, the genius
of pinks and greys and reds, the bruised
brown and olive of dung on the flanks,
the way his bedroom is crowded with
these dumb animated pigs, their eyes
staring tenderly out, as if they know
that in dreams he sees them skewered,
turning over flame. It begins with the sow
during hog-killing season, the coarse
salt, the smoke of hard hickory wood,
the slicing of flesh to be preserved
for the cold barren season; it begins
with ham hocks and grease, the crackling,
the oily curled crispy back skin
of the curing hog; it begins with
the thought of meat, the last of the salt
pork deep in February before the Lenten
season of river fish. In his dreams, a man
comes into his sty with a knife and begins
a carnival of blood, the slaughtering
of pigs, the skid and tussle in the mud,

blood and shit, the squeals like people
hurrying to the corners, pressing against
the sturdy fencing with nowhere to go;
the steam rising from his slick skin
and the heavy torsos of pigs laid out
as if waiting for piglets to come to suckle.
The stillness. A man with a butchering
knife in hand, his chest wet with blood,
circling crows and the promise of all
things ending. It begins with the murder,
begins with the noose, begins with a dick
stuffed down a throat, begins with terror,
before this art explodes around him. Left
alone, he is still on his bed; the stench
of the hog farm carrying over the open soy
fields into his room. It begins with hogs;
most things do around here, it seems.

Reburial

Sometimes a man is one same song,
that is all there is to him. Maybe it wasn't
always that way with him, maybe one time
he had a wide open brain, and tomorrow
was like a window to him, a sky
so wide you could tell that all kinds
of songs were living there.
And when you saw him coming
you didn't know what song
you would hear, because that man
had many songs. But a stone
can rise at a man's feet and cause
him to stumble, cause the world
to change, make the window
close, gather the grey and mauve
in the sky and leave him with this
one blanketing song, this shadow
over all he does. And this citizen
let a man die over stolen nails,
or broke his wife's heart with his
infidelity, or made God wink
with a constant weakness; and soon
this is his only song, the shadow
of dusk. A man like that will do
anything to learn a new song, to shake
this one song from his skin. So
he follows the instructions
of the diviner, bathes until his skin
is blistered and waterlogged, and
then he enters the sky naked
and starts to travel the magic
ship that will take him beyond

water, beyond light, deep into
the city of bones where we must
leave the unwanted things
and then pray he may return
to the surface of things, filled
with new songs and laughter.

Horse

I stole a bucket of nails. The mill wouldn't pay me so I stole a
bucket of nails. They say Garret Brown stole it he ran and jumped
in the river.

—Citizen Barlow, in *Gem of the Ocean,*
by August Wilson

The last light before dusk and the pitch
of a winter night is comfort. For days
I have sought out the sunlit places
to stand and be warmed, to burn out
the wracking chill in the body. This
ague holds you, wraps its prickly
blanket about you, and deep down
under your skin, inside your bones,
a terrible terror. My skin has
been pale as death for days. Last
night a horse with its belly gutted
open came and stood at the stone
where I rested my head; its eyes
were soft as memory while it bled
into the earth. I tried to raise my hand
to caress this clumsy head but
could not move. The horse trotted
away, leaving a trail of water
and blood in its wake. Then came
the fevers and the search for moon-
light; chasing dogs, chasing the hounds
across the tobacco fields, through
the untidy chaos of bush and tree
roots; and the dogs howling
with me chasing them, as if in them

I will find a secret. The answers
are in food. Soft-boiled food—the flesh
of yams, cassavas, boiled rice and grits.
The answers are in the soft overripe
peaches and pears, pregnant to bursting,
so long scattered under the trees they
have fermented. And so I eat
them to ward off the ache
in the bones. At the railroad tracks,
the horse has grown rotten over time.
A white sack of maggots congregates
for the feast—but oh, the head!
That beautiful head! The empty boxcar
smells of fish; the train makes no
sound; it moves under the water. I am
going to whistle a long hooting
sound to clear the way. The man
in the river waves to me, then raises
both arms before he sinks. There is
a ripple, and then nothing but the
still reflection of trees on the water's
surface. I will always carry a fistful
of nails in my pocket. A fistful of
ordinary nails. If I had a hammer . . .
wish I had a hammer, child, I wish.

Ship-Sailing

Where the blue ends, a crowd of clouds;
the arrival of storms is sudden here
where the dusty sand cakes, littered
with black seaweed—the sea is brown
with its churning; the ship rocks.
You will learn the meaning of dreams
in this house of wooden slats,
a pliant floor, windows tiny
as excuses; you will learn here
that when the wind blows, the walls
will creak. You will understand
that these acolytes, singing
prayers through the night,
are the deckhands hauling
ropes, hoisting the rusted, stained
sails, waiting for the flop of unfurling
before the wind is pocketed
in their give. You will know
the scent of the sea, here
in a Pittsburgh clapboard home;
you will learn the history
of your unbecoming, the dialect
of iron houses squealing against
the stubborn defiance of wood;
you will long for sunlight,
long for the end of storms,
long to be strapped and chained
to the mast while the battering
of so many stories weakens you.
This house is a ship setting sail.

Psalm 104

1
City

Some began with nothing but faith,
following the routes old-time slaves
used to take, keeping away from the wrath
of hounds, following the river where old graves
of the blessed sometimes gave up their bones,
along feet-hardened paths through woods.

But soon, all the bread turned to stone,
and the thirst and hunger in their blood
slowed them down; no borders here,
no counties; just the howl of wolves,
and all they had was a quick prayer
and faith in the appearance of doves.

God presented them with a city, a habitation
of brick and steel; their dubious salvation.

2
A-Sea

All these journeys over dry pampas, the salvages
where the leaves swallow salt and thrive;
everything turns white as bone; our baggage
weighs us down—the boat will arrive,
its belly low on the water. The merchants
calculate our worth.

At mid sea
we learn to read the sky, to search its scant
blankness for hints, before the heave
of waves—this is the glory of the Lord.

This journey is a return to the familiar
terror of the sea and the Almighty's rod
taming us. This is the path travelers
take to the city of bones in the deep,
where, at last, the traveler will sleep.

3
Mother

A motherless mother knows the breaking of loss,
carries it in the slope of her shoulders, the way
she stands on the beach after the heave and toss
of the long crossing; a thousand souls pray
for the language to hope, their sour breaths
blowing into the sails; the sound is a cry
that has no reply.

We did not arrive with stealth,
we arrived emptied of what we had tried
all along the journey to keep dry and whole—
the memories, the songs. But under the shadow
of whooping sails, the air sucks deep holes
into the body, leaving you to seep that slow
seepage of despair.

I, mother of thousands,
am still trying to retrieve those healing songs.

4
Stole

Ole pirates yes they rob I
Stole I to the merchant ship
—Bob Marley

So funny how the path to redemption songs
is crowded with the questions only sufferers
ask—Why? What did we do, and for how long?—
as if their perdition marks the measure
of how fallen they have been. The truth
is always harder: all are broken people;
everyone has some secret, some uncouth
narrative of failure. But how terrible
must one's sins be to cause such ugliness?
These chains, these dungeons, this hole,
this enslavement, this distress,
this loss of all things holy, all they stole
from us. If it is not the fault of the slave,
who will cry out when they dance on his grave?

5
Iron

Before your journey across the steaming earth
towards the water's edge, before you step in,

feel the tickling warmth slowly washing dirt
from your salt-dry skin; check for everything.

Make sure you have a flask of rainwater,
the knotted torso of a ginger root; a flower

that broke out of a brittle shell; a piece of paper
with simple verbs scrawled all over

its plain surface—and a piece of iron, as old
as you can find. The man who makes this journey

without iron will soon falter, will grow cold
at the sight of the city of bones; his body

will shiver with fever; and the congregation
will sing softly: "Too late, too late for heaven."

6
Ginger

Peel the ginger of its pale skin, let the white
bone show; a touch of green is good, it is hope.

Chop the flesh; breathe the soft quiet
healing in the broken parts; if you can cope
with the bite of sun, you can cope with loss.

Put the handful of broken ginger in a pot
of water; let it boil long, slow, until it mists
and the root grows soft. Place your face over the hot
pot; breathe some more, till sweat covers you.

Now pour off the juice, crush the root, squeeze
your fist around the pulp. A lime and two
palms full of brown sugar stirred in, then let breeze

cool your brew, let it settle for three days;
then drink slowly; purge your history away.

7
Flack

For days it has been raining a brittle cold deluge
slicking the streets; even the horses have been
dragging their buggies with haste to find refuge
in warm stables. I have seen
in this twilight the rain stippling the eastern window-
panes, your lithe body, a brown glow against
the pewter grey of the sky, your scarf a glow,
as you collect the bucket, now full of rain.
And you have come in smelling of sweat
and the biting salt of sex, poured the cold water
into my soldier's flask, your eyes wet
with the laughter of the satisfied. I grow hard
again with gratitude as you soak a blue rag
and cool my brow and say, "Ah, my love, my stag."

8
Comfort

We quarrel as if we have forgotten already the taste
of our skins, the way in the midst of our lovemaking
we stopped, holding our breaths as if not to waste
this moment with labor, as if in that halting
we were afraid to imagine anything else but
the perfect completion of desire and death.

Even the word "love" seemed facile for this gut-
churning vertigo, this wordless sucking out of breath,
before we howled so loudly, so riotously,
that we frightened even ourselves. Now we argue
as if we have places to run away to angrily,
as if in the desert of absence we would have a clue

of how to live without each other. I offer
this craven comfort: to love like this is to suffer.

9
City of Bones

At the gate to the city of splendor, the city
of beauty, light as an open doorway,
the broken darkness of the hull, there's no pity;

just the gatekeeper whose name you say
with soundless gulps, for the gatekeeper
is the one you have wounded, the dark

memory waiting to lash out. You fall deeper
into your sorrow with the offering of the stark
nakedness of your plea for mercy. You

will sweat at the city of bones, tremble
at the bone-weary ache in your body,
and when you beg for mercy, you will stumble
into the brilliant impossible of silver
in this gleaming city of celestial splendor.

PART FOUR

City of Bones

Prelude

> I caught a dove darkening the dawn
> with her brooding,
> grieving the loss of the cold ark.
> I let her fly near the light
> of the bright green lime tree,
> the steaming red hibiscus.
>
> —Esther Phillips, "Bird Catcher"

The sun falls out of heaven like a stone;
a network of bridges sprouts over the rivers;
so many tunnels bite deep into the hills
like bridges connecting these islands of houses
teetering on the side of the undulating hills.
A dark stain in the sky smells of iron;
you can see the gleam of steel packed
on the barges nosing towards the Ohio.

In the boarding house a man—a round,
plump little black man—dances
with quiet dignity while holding
the soft tremor of a pigeon in his hands.
He blows a spray of whiskey
in its curious eye. Soon it is drunk
with revelations, the bones slipping.

The conjure man has learned
the vocabulary of leaves and roots,
the dialog of blood. He breaks
the neck with common mercy;
spills the blood in an enamel cup
with its brown cracks and chipped
lip; he makes a circle in the earth,

scoops up dirt, lays the pigeon
out, wing to wing as if in flight.

From here you can't hear the drum
pounding in the air, can't see
the flame of light on his skin,
can't understand the crowd of words
spilling rapidly from his mouth,
but you imagine that his black knife
with its silver edge has split
open so many breasts to find the green,
pink and red entanglement of visions.

If you look closely into the slippery
viscera, you will see a thin mist
rising like mysteries he must read.
Then he covers the inert corpse
with dirt, and as if to fulfill
the promise of resurrection, he pours
the blood over the upturned earth,
and raises his eyes from the earth
over the stand of pine trees,
across the mountains, then east over
the Monongahela, going home,
going home. The fat squat man
stands, spreads his arms, and
in this instance you know
he too can fly, that he can lift
himself, dusty coat and hat,
and rise, soaring, soaring, soaring.

The Way of the World

For Roger Guenveur Smith

1

There is a universe of history
caught in this nondescript
boarding house: such small
lives; the dispensability of migrants
counting pennies, imagining
dreams; a death with boots on,
a night with lamplight,
meat swimming in a pot;
a universe of race caught
in the reliable timber and plaster
of this boarding house.

2

Here, in between centuries—
first trauma, the chaos
of dysfunction, before the shock
of mass bloodletting—these black
folk have long understood
the insanity of living; Jack
Johnson grinning over the flattened
body of a white man; Reverend
Dixon, that South Carolina
gentleman unearthing the demons
of a nation's waywardness,
and oh, the starched white

hoods, the thunder hoofs,
the snug efficiency of a noose;
a universe of understanding
in the flight to find order
in the promise of wages,
here at the edge of the abyss.

3

Old Mr. Smith sometimes dreams
he sees his grandchildren still
there in Georgia; dreams of collards
and fatback, dreams of the way
the sin can grow over you like
a ball and make you say, "Jesus!"
But he won't go back, not ever.
Somebody is waiting at the border
because he knows he stole
himself and two hundred dollars
worth of debt from those Bowdens
when he slipped out at night,
lied to his woman, lied to
himself, and walked for days,
his heart thumping in his chest,
until he could make it here;
so he can't go back—nobody
can go back. This is the way
of the world, he says,
this is the way of the world.

Father Poem

When your father comes to you in that land
of big things, you must duck the giant
sparrow and find shelter beneath dwarfing
trees. Still, he will follow you, talking,
talking in a voice that you will know.
And as he comes closer to you, you will
smell his sweat and know it as yours,
the same old oil-heavy sweat you smelt
rising out of the pine box where he lay
for a day and night waiting for the horses
to leave the settlement; waiting for those too-
drunk crackers to tire of hunting
down some daring soul; waiting for church
to call. We kept the curtains shut,
kept the candles cold while your father
wouldn't say a word, the blood
drying on his shirt to a deep
shit brown. But he is clean as a body
should be here in this land of big
things, and his arms are long and thick,
and his mouth bigger than a wide-
brimmed hat, and you can't stop
him talking and waving those arms;
and he is telling you things he never
would say all those years he would
grunt and mumble and thumb
directions for you; so if he says
find your own song because you are singing
other people's songs for too long, then you must
listen; and if he says, "Look for the *shining
man*," you must listen, and even when
you go blind like his father did from the light,

and you can't find your way back to your
father with his big mouth and fat hands,
you will carry this hunger and confusion
all your life, and you will give
yourself a name and a purpose,
blood on your hands and your face,
a new song gurgling in your throat.

Biscuits

Most of God's blessings are simple:
a pot of grits, a cup of coffee,
and some golden-brown biscuits
made with a quart of sifted flour,
a tablespoon of salt, a teaspoon
of soda, a mess of lard,
a pint of sour milk, and just
to let people know where to come
back for more, a taste
of molasses. Now, you shorten
that into a banty-egg size
before you roll that out
and cut them up into half
a fist. Don't grease the pan,
just watch the wood so it
cook slow and easy, till
you can smell that sweetness
a mile away; and that is
God's blessing; and these hands
know how to make a traveling
soul feel as if maybe tomorrow
they will find their lost love,
or find a job, or find
a quarter on the road, or, if
they are lucky, find their
song that they lost so long
ago when they left the farm
to find something else.

Lost

Poem for Mattie

There is no magic to finding the lost;
they are somewhere, and where they are
is the history of who we were,
and so it is not them you are missing
but you—like a song you are singing
and then it stops in your brain
and you want to finish it, but you
can't, not until you find the lost soul.

People leave mostly in the dead
of night. It just takes a word
or the way a white man looks
at you, or sometimes you see it
in the preacher's face, a kind
of dead music as if to say there's
nothing here for you anymore.

You learn quickly that the extent
of what you know is not all you have,
and when the roads don't look
familiar, and the trees start to turn
an alien shade of green, and when
you can't read the clouds anymore,
you know the world is bigger
than your eyes, bigger by far.

They leave nothing behind,
and all you have is the trail
of people they came by, said
hello, made a joke or two,

but people travel with no name,
no destination—you find
the next town, stop, see if someone
will give you work; and your face
feels new, as if you've been born again
when you see it in a mirror.

This man gets caught up in some mess;
tomorrow he is on the chain gang,
and he will come back home to find
nothing but dry cornstalks and a debt
bigger than his life. This man will
change his name, walk until he knows
his face has changed, too, and he
will carry in him the end of a story.

No magic in finding the lost ones;
they are somewhere; they are waiting
for someone to say, "I know your
face, I know your face," and that
is when they will say, "I have
the rest of your story, if you want it."

Making Love in a Boarding House

Everything complains in this house; you
sleep in the spaces between snores;
your body knows the rhythm of others;
and to make love, you must stand,
brace yourself against the wall, let
him bend his knee just so you can
meet, and when you have met, he
will carry you; and everything must
be slow, the crooked dance between
people whose only light is the moon.
And if he steps, stamps his feet,
he must keep on stamping his
feet like he is dancing; and if
you make a sound in your throat
you must sing a holy hymn
all the way; and as the startling
noise of your arrivals covers you,
you must lock teeth into each
other's lips and bite for dear life,
bite for salt, bite for tears
to run down your faces, bite
as if a bit has been stuffed
in your mouth to stanch
the scream of a whip falling
wet and long across the back;
bite and hold on, and let
all the music of the night
surround you, until you are trembling flesh,
a humming woman, a stamping man,
between snores, between the giggles

in the walls, between the groans
of the timber straining against the night;
between the rustle of leaves,
you find yourselves in silences, and
there politely whisper your gratitude.

Desperation

To be loved hard is to crowd your head
with the craziness of desperation.
No matter how you think you have turned
this thing into an ordinary transaction,
desire and hunger meet—an understanding;
hard love will come on you and you
won't know where to go. Everybody
knows where to find a binding man,
and if you don't, you should know
who cooks your red stew, see what
they put in it, know all the signs
that your woman has grown desperate.
She will stop talking, stop quarreling,
stop asking about your going out
and coming in; she will pray more,
put her hand on you casually,
her head slick with oil, just touching
your skin, making your body sting
with confusion. Sometimes, you
will open your eyes and catch her
looking at you as if she is searching
for the words she has lost in you
a long time ago. And she won't
look away, just stare at you,
her face a mask of neutrality.
She will step out late at night
and come back with dew darkening
the edge of her skirt and her face glowing
with sweat. She will read your mind,
and, for the first time, you will know
what a book feels like, or what it is like
to have the Holy Ghost look at you.

And every plan you have made to pack
up and walk away, every deal you've
struck, every lie you've told, will
grow nervous inside you. It won't be
long before you can tell that you
are dead without her, and you can't
move, can't step away, can't escape
her cold, stern face. That is how you
know that she has bound on earth
what the spirit binds in heaven.
And just when you accept it all,
you will see that she has found
nothing happy in this triumph, just
the bitter fatalism of a ball and
chain tied around her ankle.

Possession

Sunday morning, you find your song;
it grows in you in the dark place of prayer,
your body battered by the thump of tambourines
and stumping feet; you are watching for God
to come like wind into the congregation,
but tarrying so long; it starts up
with the empty silence, like a barefaced
sky, inscrutable and cloudless, and here
every detail of living comes crowding
in; and the more you wait, the more
you think of your flesh, of the memory
in the ache of your thighs of some
transgression—the tough knot
in your palm's heel that planted
too hard a blow; all the frustration
of waiting for hope rising under
your skin. You know your sin,
you know your doubt; you forget
the path to peace and hallelujah
a week ago. But all yesterdays
are lies; today, this morning
in the creaking coffin of a sanctuary,
is all you have, all you have
to feed you for tomorrow, and you
know that if you take a breath
and blow it out, your heart will
start to push, and if you groan
for love to conquer you, your feet
will start to move; and the thing
hits your belly and the sky grows
bigger, a chaotic clamor of clouds
thickening the light to a soup

of grey-green; and you start
to call the name, say the name,
sing the name until your words
collide and convulse, and your
throat knows that what is in
your belly is more than *Jesus!*—more
than *Jeeee-sus!*—more than *Oh!*—
more than *Oh!*—more than the
language you have learned about
the earth; it is a sound bigger
than your tongue. And as it
heaves in you, your throat opens
and the storm of disaster explodes;
the alarum of arrival consumes
you and the fire that holds
your head is the fire of a body
twisting against the wind;
and Sunday morning is as holy
as the common lily in the field.

Plot

A heavy-tongued man arrives at dusk
with a little girl on his arm; he says
little, says he is looking for a woman
called Hallelujah. It is the search for
a runaway woman that begins a plot.
No one knows what he wants to do
when he finds her, no one knows
why he is looking for her. Some of us
sitting in the backyard, staring
at fireflies darting in the dark,
imagine a brute stabbing, a body
stretched out on grass, her hands
facing upwards, a question on her
stiff mouth. We think of him, too,
breaking down before her, weeping,
bleeding for another chance. And someone
mentions the man she must be with now,
perhaps a preacher, or a welder,
or a stonebreaker. They think of him
taking a bullet in the face, falling
on his back, inert, shocked at how
easily death can come. We do
not know; our night is livid with stories
of what might be, the psychosis
of a man who has traveled hundreds
of miles, through North Carolina,
across West Virginia, then across
the Potomac into the thick green
hills of Maryland, before the clean
skies of Pennsylvania—walking,
dust-laden, eyes sodden with sorrow
and the madness of hunger; walking

with this child at his side, asking strangers,
"Have you seen, have you seen, have you seen?"
and expecting someone to have seen. An old
trickster prophesies blindly the rules
of finding, the laws of following,
the calculation of binding and release.
There are those cursed to be together,
and that is a hex that can be bought.
When a person is hexed and is bound,
one day she will know she hates
what she is bound to, but can't leave
without torture of her soul. Still
she will go, and the left one will
follow. So the man wants to find
this woman who left him with a girl.
Somebody knows this woman;
she knows somebody; this is
how a story starts, and the drama
is in seeking what has been lost.

Scent

A man studies the trail of smoke in the sky—
in this swelling city a cluster of mountain
settlements. He has learned how to sniff the air
in search of the things he has lost. Deep
in the underbelly of the nation, the swamp
air is thick, carries scents sluggishly, and after
a while, after pushing your nose into the wind,
you learn how to separate a chicken stew
dinner from the gummy sweetness of bubbling
grits, or the green mugginess of steamed collards.

You know your own stink, can tell when
rain is coming and how soon. You grow
alert like a hound dog slinking against a peeling
fence. This is what is lost when you travel;
every place smells different, and the grass
and trees speak a different language. Further
north, the air is clean of all remembering,
and the man carries in his sack the worn
brown frock of his woman, the one
he imagines still smells of her, the one
he has bundled as his pillow night
after night, until their sweat has mingled,
and now they are one thick scent.

At night, he gathers it to his face and smells her,
to remember her, as weeks turn to months,
and months to a year, and if he were honest
he would say she is fading, and all he smells
is the funk of his desire and bitterness
on those miles of miles of sky they have walked
looking for her. He waits until morning,
lifts his face, prays for a right wind
to blow her onion-and-thyme scent to him.

Moses Houser

She named him for a woman—a name
old as trees. They took him to the cotton
tree root, buried his slippery navel string,
raised him high and called his name
three times: "Moses, Moses, Moses."
And in their heads this boy would
turn into a man who could take all
these scattered folks, following along
dusty roads criss-crossing a blasted
land, everyone counting the dead,
everything upside down: in Charleston,
negroes speechifying in the state house;
in Columbia, black folks graduating
from university, heads high—not everyday
negroes, but those high-colored negroes
who always knew that their time
would come. And while they prance and mince,
white folks are scratching out a living
like slaves in the fields razed to dry pampas
by the vengeful orders of Sherman.

But the poor old slave people have to
keep moving, looking for work, looking
for each other, looking for somewhere
to run to, looking to build villages
where at last they could be far
from white people, far enough
for this boy, Moses, to only know
good hearts, decent ways, strong,
proud people. They named their babies
Abraham, or some rebirthed their family;
threw off some slave name for Jackson,
or Washington; and this prayer was
on his head when he stomped down

a drunk white man, when he ran
like a prophet up North to find a burning
bush, to live long enough to gather
his voice and return to lead all these
exiled people, these careless Ethiopians, home.

But Moses Houser used to stand
on the bridge and look upriver
to another bridge, and to another,
and he could not stop his mind from
going back to the way that cracker
took his woman from him, simple
as a meal and room, left him there
with his two long arms, wondering
what Moses Houser must do next.

It was no surprise to those who found
him entangled in the marshes and reeds,
his body grey and swollen, but his eyes
closed like prayer. He was not right
in the head, never was, always dreaming.
He decided to fly, just one time,
to skim the surface of the river, to clear
one bridge and find another, to fly
and fly until he could fly no more.

Relief

For Molly

A mile away, I could not calm the thick
cloud of sadness in my throat—what I
have left behind, the runs, the drunken
quarrels, the failure of love. Lord, I tried,
but I knew it was dead so long ago,
and then he hits me again as if to tell
me to go away, like a dying man
telling the other survivors to go on;
like good slave, Onesimus, too tired to continue,
knowing that the others will be caught
by the catchers if they try to hold
him. He hit me like that, with tender
in his eyes, telling me to go, and I
carry that news in my chest
until I come to the boarding house,
and I want to be told welcome,
'cause my ankles ache, and my
bladder is full, and I have not
seen a bed for days, I have not
had a regular meal for days,
and my body is gritty with dirt
off the road, and the deep stench
of sweat and sadness. So see how
quickly the smell of day-old sweet
bacon and fresh biscuits can turn
my stomach soft with hope; how
quickly this landlord's stern arrangements
(dollar a week, twenty-five cents
for meals, two meals a day, no

bad living, no mess) can reassure
me that there is some order in the world;
how the young boy tenant looks
at my body and you can see in his
eyes days of constant sunshine,
like he has been happy before—
dumb happy, crazy happy, like
a long dive into river water, like
laughing so deep it hurts, takes
my breath from me, makes
me wet myself—like he has
had dreams that have shadowed him
with sweetness for days, and days—
the recalibration of his days right
there. Now that makes the pressure
in my bladder, makes me start
to shuffle and talk fast with a smile;
and I know he heard me say I want
to have company, Lord, I want to have
my own key, and my own door,
and my own air to smell of me,
my own self—I know he heard me,
and felt the breeze of need
as I hurried past to find the outhouse
where I could let the steam
of all this holding back burst,
my skin pimpling, my eyes warm
with relief, the summer turning green.

Haircut

A quick scissors is an art: the clip and cool
press to the hum and wheezing of a man
who will turn an entanglement of thick
knots into the fine veneer of shade
over a gleaming pate. Hair is his
medium, and you trust the slow
gentle tumble of clumps down your
face, the sharp shards of white hair
where the quick swishing of the blades
comes close to throat, close to skin.

You will carry scars for life
at the hands of a careless barber,
but a skillful artist will draw
pimples of blood, but never leave
a mark; this is about trust,
this is how men learn to trust men
for their skill, their art, their devotion
to a job well done like ritual.
Still a barber owns your life;
he is close to the flesh. In the back-
yards, ritual of turning, long-road
travelers, rough-headed plantation
runaways, scraggly unwilling
beards in clumps,
a man who looks wild and withered
as the terror behind him, will sit
to feel the gentle pull and nudge
of knuckles and hooked fingers
under the chin, the thrust of torso
against a shoulder to guide the body;
feel the cooling of the scalp

before the open caress of a whipping
brush; and he will stand,
unburdened, his head catching light,
reminded of what it is like
to start all over again with the remains
of his memory strewn about his feet.

Come and Go

For the generations of "people finders"

I have seen them come and go,
some of them dusty and tough-skinned
with yellow eyes as alert as a mongrel's.
Grin and they grin back—we call
them chattel. I have seen them.
It is easy to mistreat them; they have
no fight left in them. 100 slaves inherited,
you count them as your security,
though more fickle than the dime-an-acre
land stretching across the Piedmont,
but dear, dear, dear on the block.
They come and go. Finding the lost
ones, the running ones, is in my
blood. My father could see
the fidget in a negro long before
he knew himself he wanted to run;
and if you think like one, think
of what it is like to feel as if
the world ends beyond the county
line, if you understand that
running is an act of leaving
but not arriving, because all
there is is faith in someplace
else, you can find them, shivering
under a bush, all the fight
sweated out of them. This is
what my father taught me,
and he would begin by saying,
"Repeat after me: Dred Scott, that

nigger, is your friend—don't you
forget that; Dred Scott, and the judge,
Roger Bubba Taney, they is your
money in the bank." They come
and go because they have only
this place and the rest is somewhere
to move from when they arrive. Here
in Pittsburgh, they come, edgy, eyes
yellow with fear, and I know
how to find them, how to track
them down, especially the lost
ones, sitting on a tree stump,
looking as if they have forgotten
their names, always staring
at the road; those who look
up and far when they hear
the train coming; those who
grow quiet as death when
they hear the train going.
They are always coming and
going; that is all they have
and I can sniff them out.
It is as simple as that.

The Separation/Retention

It should be as African as possible .
> —August Wilson, stage directions for performing the
> juba, in *Joe Turner's Come and Gone*

How African can it possibly be to dance
to the flattened palms on a wooden table,
to be belly full of fried chicken and sweet
potatoes, to be blood dizzy with sugared
tea, to be shuffling on the creaking boards,
to be circling around a round, fat conjure
man calling out the dip and spin, a man
whose gift and calling is to bind
lost and fleeing souls? How African
could it be to shuffle like this into
a frenzy, to lose decorum in the waist,
to sweat, to abandon the pressure
of your daily worries, to forget the long
road ahead of you, to make your
body release all the mourning
in your heart for what you have
left behind; to make a pattern
of twists and turns that batter
down every longing, every need
you have for a touch, every
hunger unmet? How African could
it be? Only the long gash
of forgetting, the shame of remembering,
the empty space where language
was, the transition of self
and meaning into the lowest form
of ignorance; only the stiff collar
of a preacher's sermon against

the hand rising up inside of you;
only the fear of spirits on dark
dusty roads, only the burden
of your grandmother's smell,
like the smell of a deep forest;
only the yellow of her eyes, the heaviness
of her tongue, the gutturals she speaks
into the night; only the dread
of that, the fear of losing yourself
to something beyond you, yet
deep inside of you; only
the auctioneer's scatology,
the commerce of your labor;
only this seductive love called
America with its cold breath
on you despite its promises of warmth;
only these could make it impossible
to be African. How African can
this juba dance be, how African?

The Size of God

If God is bigger than everything a man has,
then a man is nothing and every spirit-crushing
story whispered in his ear becomes true.

The wandering man walks with a spirit riding
him, keeps on telling him that God is a wall
and a wall will not listen. The man asks
the wall why his woman has left him
and the wall does not speak. The man
stands naked in an open field and looks

at the creature in his hand, a monstrosity
that grows into grand sleekness
at his touch; he holds it in his fist
and moves his hand until his shoulders
hunch, and the sun batters his head;

the hawks dart above and he thinks
in that sharp light of his coming
that he is bigger than the Holy Ghost,
this heavy firm swelling in his hand
will frighten the world to pray,

he, a convulsing creature spewing
rivers. The dreams he has stretched
out on the grass and flattened dry
cornstalks are of bones climbing
out of water, bones walking on water,

the sea rising and covering the army
of bones, then vomiting them out again
onto the shore, these bones now

covered in flesh—black still bodies
strewn on the beach waiting for the wind.

Now he is stretched on the beach
waiting for the wind, the limp
amphibian of his penis panting
on his belly. It is night when the wind
blows, and God is in the wind
filling him, filling the strewn bodies.

They rise slowly, worming to the road,
not knowing where to go, but going.

Molly's People

1

Six healthy children and a day to day,
but this man will not be satisfied
because in his head the world's way
should have an answer for every cry he's cried
for what is righteous. This man, this basic
black man, just freshly free from slavery,
wants to set the world right, to trick
every demon out to eat into his bravery
with a plain song, a rising plain song.
This man is jittery all the time,
staring out at the road, waiting for so long,
wanting to tell people, "Freedom is no crime."
Try to live with such a man and you will
suffer, because a man like that can't get his fill.

2

Her mother taught her how to watch for the signs—
the greening in the skin, the complaint
of a sour thirst every morning, the lines
cutting into the lips and the blotchy stains
all over the skin; and she taught her
to count the months before the belly
distended, poking out of his tight shirt
and waistcoat. They called it scurvy,
but her mother knew better, knew
the bitterness she stewed in the pot
for those white folks would make them blue
in the gills eventually. "Learn the rot

in hurt people; don't eat from their hand;
be watchful always for the killing poisons."

3

Run as she might from North Carolina's
tobacco fields, from her daddy's restless
ways, from the quarrels, words of bitter
regret, never satisfied till a great mess
is made of everything good around him;
run as she tries from her mother's suspicion
of every neighbor's gaze or soft hand,
of every stray wind and every notion
hanging around their hometown, she
finds herself traveling with an uneasy heart,
a contrary soul, constantly wary
of every kindness on the way. Her path
is always the quarrelsome way,
her way of keeping her enemies at bay.

If You Know Her

If you know your woman, know her rhythms,
know her ways, if you've paid attention
to her all these years, you will know
how she comes and goes, how she slips
away even though she is standing in
the same place; you will know that her
world is drifting softly from you, and she
may not mean it, because all it is
is she is scared to be everything, scared
to be finding herself in you every time,
scared that one day she will ask herself,
all forty-plenty years of her, where
she's been; if you know your woman,
you will know that mostly she will
come back, but sometimes when she
drifts like this, something can make her
slip, and then coming back is hard.
She will buy some leather boots
and not say a word about it,
and you only see them when she walks
in one night, and she says she's had
them forever. You will see the way
she loses the weight and pretends
it's nothing, but when she isn't seeing you
looking, you see how she faces the mirror,
lifts her chest to catch a profile,
and casually looks at her
ass for signs of life. If you know
your woman, when you are gone, she
will find things to do like walk
alone, go see a movie, find a park,

collect her secrets and you won't know,
because she is looking for herself.
She won't tell you that she wants
to hear what idle men say when she
walks by them, because what you say
is not enough. If you know your
woman, you know when she's going
away and you will feel the big
hole of your love, and you can't
tell why she's listening and humming
to tunes you did not know she heard
before, and she will laugh softly
at nothing at all. If you know your
woman, you will see how she comes
and goes, and all you can do is wait
and pray she will come back to you,
because you know that your sins
are enough for her to leave and not return.

Avoiding the Spirits

I don't play that piano cause I don't want to wake them spirits.
They never be walking around in this house.
                        —Berniece, in *The Piano Lesson*, by August Wilson

When, at sunset, the congregation gathers
in the low light of St. Helena's old grey
Baptist chapel, they guard their hearts
from the whisper of the low-bellied trees,
calling on the blood as they brush off
the dew on their coats by the burial ground.
When they sing, the sound has the flat
simplicity of prayer, a sound that brings
heat to your neck, tears to your eyes,
because you can hear in the rugged
rafters, hewn from old-growth trees
at the water's edge, the voices of all those
people who had nothing but lament
and Jesus to fill the gap of a stolen life.
The sisters can't make a man cross
that threshold unless he has come
to lay someone to rest or to witness
a child's blessing or a daughter's
wedding, for a man can't hear the flat
voices in the church and not feel
the droop of his shoulders
and the weight of his dangling
empty hands that have too often
hung helpless for prudence's sake, for good
sense, making him not a man,
but an empty shell, a creature
who laughs to stop the shame
of not being able to keep his family

together and safe. No, he will rather
sit in the dark cathedral of the juke
joint and let the blues of sardonic
regret and caustic distance
wash him, make him know that
he is alone on the road, and all
he's got is his story. My people
long gave up on the ancestors
when they learned that those
stepping out of the woods
are the crippled gods, the beaten
gods, the blackened and burnt-out
tongueless gods, the broken
gods, the castrated gods, the shadow
gods with questions, asking
us if they will ever heal, asking
for a balm from the living. Who wants
to pour libation for the burdened
spirits? Silence is our salvation,
that and the reassurance of this earth,
this clear air, this forgetting.

Profit

and this is why we find
however deep we listen
that the skies are silent
        —Don Paterson, "The Error"

The art of profit is the art of unbelief.
Take a roots man; he must draw out of people
the conviction that each herb steeped
in hot water, each leaf, oil crushed out
on pestle and mortar, can turn the direction
of the wind, can beat back the thick
hatred in the hearts of one's enemies—all
this to turn a profit—no, not even a profit;
all this to make a soul give coin,
offer money out of gratitude for the earnest
of things hoped for. The basic landlord
counts the days, bars of soap, meals eaten,
linen used before the washing; he knows
to ask for cash in advance, knows
that a body that disappears after
paying the rent is a profitable body;
knows that he needs no prayers
to find a body hungry for a meal,
for the comfort of a wooden dining table,
for the ritual of a shelter at night.
He builds only. What he has of worth
is land, the basic equations of the earth.
This is the art of profit, and he knows
that when he falls flat on his back,
the solid gift of his land will continue
to give. This man does not speak
to the sky; it is, after all, an emptiness

that offers only the occasional grumbling,
rain and snow and the patterns
of random luck. Profit is in the earth,
the reliability of brick and mud, the tough
language of debt and payments.

Joe Turner

For August Wilson

How many women across the Bible Belt
have learned in their hearts the old song
of the strutting man who has cut a swath
through tobacco and cotton fields, deep into
the rice swamps and indigo groves, over by
the sawmills and lumberyards, up in those
textile factories breathing out smoke and dust?
He has gone into the villages at the edge
of the country where black men play dominoes
and count out the hours, sipping liquor
and spitting tobacco juice; gone down to the back
trails with the sun-warm juke joints
where the blues is all the healing left
for men whose eyes have grown deep
as rivers, seen so much, taken so much
that their faces are sun-leathered masks
you can't read; good men, broken men,
men leaving late-night hallelujah
meetings, their hearts swollen with
the Holy Ghost who has told them
their new names, their man names.

A swaggering white man has come
down to where black men are tasting the salt
in their sweat, learning the funk
in their seed as they try to be men.
He has come and gathered them up
with the law, dragged them to the hole
to be judged by good white deacons and trustees,

night riders, Carolina's Reverend Dixon's
heroes, and Anglo-Saxon farming
men who were broken apart by the blights
consuming all whites after the Civil War.
He has brought the black men here
to be judged by these white men
who are just now finding back the dignity they lost
during those dark days of the seventies
and eighties when the nappy-haired,
uppity, ignorant, broad-nosed, and vengeful-
hearted negro upstarts thought they could be
equal to these white heroes of America.

Yes, this swashbuckling, big-gutted,
clear-eyed man has come back
to find the idle, the runaway, the violent,
the sassy, the disrespectful; and people
know his name at Parchman, Angola—
these women have a song for him:
Joe Turner, Joe Turner's come and gone!
Joe Turner, Joe Turner's come and gone!
He comes when they are not looking,
comes when their eyes are elsewhere,
comes like a thief in the night, comes
like the old slave catchers,
like the auctioneers, like those square stern ships
sliding over the hot-faced sea, *Joe Turner,*
Joe Turner, Joe Turner's come and gone!

Mama Ola Speaks

1

All these men and boys, muscles growing hard,
but their hearts drying up—these men and boys,
centuries of them, each one drawing bad cards,
finding themselves broken, bodies destroyed
by these walls.   It is so hard to know
your own voice in the shadow of fences
and barbed wire. This barren place you go
out in the daytime, looking to commence
the ritual song; but you open your mouth
and all that comes out is dry, dry dust
and foul air.   Without a song, next month
is a lie you have been told; your limbs rust
in the soul-sucking air of these dusty grounds,
not a song to be heard, not a single sound.

2

You can read the mark of a slowed-down
man if you look carefully. He mostly
grows old without a fuss; even the ground
he stands on will tell you how costly
it is to heal a man who has been
broken like this. Generations have come
and gone—men who know the stain
left in them when they are seen as dumb,
helpless animals. You have one choice:
slaughter another and drink his blood

or let your song go dry, no noise
in your throat, no peace, nothing good
left in you. I pray for my songless boys,
pray they will find their stolen voice.

3

Everybody has picked some cotton some-
time; everybody walking blindly along
these twisting roads looking for their home
even though they left their home so long
ago that they have forgotten what it feels
like to be home. Plantations went to pot,
cornrows turned to nappy locks, the fields
of cotton got caught up with weed and rot,
and the roofs are falling in. This is freedom,
and people are walking, leaving old folk
like me as if we are the reason
for their sadness, as if it's we who took
from them their names. No, until you learn
to look at me, your soul will surely burn.

Touch

I done forgot how to touch.
                —Herald Loomis, in *Joe Turner's Come and Gone*,
                        by August Wilson

These hands have learned to callus against
the rub and press of wood, learned
not to feel the prickly back of cotton balls,
the chiggers feeding on the soft in between
the toes; these hands know how to hold
the neck of a hog so strong and firm
it begs for a knife, breathless, sound-
less; these hands don't even know
the history of each scar and scab, so long
they have been painless, touchless.

One time, these hands could feel
the press of guitar strings in the dark,
could feather over gentle fabric
and know the breath of silk or
fresh cotton washed to a softness
for a baby; these hands could cradle
the fragile bones of an infant,
feel the curl and wet soft hold
of her finger, wanting to touch;
to thumb into the curves and sinks
in her skull and know what
a universe of life they were holding.

These hands were once the cradle
for a woman's face, but now,
after seven years of careless
toil, seven years of heavy labor,

seven years of holding things that
don't give back—chains, stones,
shovels, cutlass, iron bars—
and his own blunt skin,
they have forgotten how to touch,
forgotten how to feel the warmth
of living under another's skin.

Equations

The calculation is simple enough;
he comes for you when you least expect,
when you are minding your own business
in the middle of a pecan grove, shells
at your feet, the sweet rot of overripe
fruit, birds feasting all about, and
suddenly, like light, he rests on you
and you think that all this dirt
you feel, all the lies you have told,
all the ways your body has gone—
breaking bones, pressing against
a woman harder than she wants it—
all that filth will fall away
if you wade out into the water.
And Jesus is the white man
at the end of the road where
the two roads cross, and he is
clean as anyone who has a bath
made for him every afternoon
at three o'clock with bath salts,
with a white towel, soft from
a well-water scrub. And he talks
to you, tells you to come follow,
and you follow because he has
you bound, tied up. And you work
for him, pick cotton for him,
plow the land for him, plant
seed for him, scare away crows
for him, and he promises you
that you won't die, never die,
that you will always be whole
like this, that he will always feed

you, always give you a suit of clothes,
always anoint you with holy oil
in the sanctuary, and your cup
runneth over, and over, and over,
and all you have to do is pick
his cotton, clear his land, make
him shine. Eventually you do
the calculation and you figure
two oughts are oughts, and you
figure that Jesus should be satisfied
now, that your bones are hurting
deep down now, that the clothes
you are wearing are worn out,
that heaven forever doesn't look
like a good idea. A pot of liquor,
some rotgut, and you see the way
the world will end, and dying
is like sleeping, but better because
you don't know. That is when you
curse Jesus and watch how his neck
pimples and turns all red, how he loses
his soft in his throat, and how
when he calls your name, it cuts
across the sky like lightning.
So you run, like any sensible nigger
will run, looking for the North Star,
leaving this piss-ass, godforsaken state
behind, so you can get some peace and rest.

Smile

He said, "I don't want you to lose your way
in my smile, baby." And he forgot where
he was and laughed. And Bertha stepped
around the kitchen, opening her palms
over the table, the stove, the pots, the pans,
and a laugh as fat as a dark wind turning
around a hill and coming down the river-
side where the bodies were still dripping
came over them. First it is the laughing,
and the belly opens up and the groin gets
loose, and the body folds in, and the tears
rush on you; when you open your arms
wide and let your throat howl its
laughter, the happy ending has come,
because he knows he is lost
in the sight of her smile, like
the hint of an oiled thigh while she
is pulling up a wayward leg of
hose, a smile bright like the smooth
glint of her underarm when she
reaches for an old pot in the corner,
and he is lost in it, not like he
has been lost before, when he did
not know his name or if he would
find his way back home—here he
is lost at his beginning, the place
of laughing, and Bertha has blessed them
with laughing, just a gift to pass through
life with. He knows this is the ending,
the place where the shining man walks
out of the dark, blood on his chest,
blood on his face, a long gleaming

knife in his bloody hand; but no one
is dead, no one but the man he left
behind; and his laugh shakes off
the shadow of the dark, and everyone
can see that he is shining. There is
nothing else for her to do, that woman with
the sweet smile, the full woman
whose man up and left her one day
without looking back, the woman
with a smile that can be a maze
of interlocking roads leading to a soft
place where roses line the neat
avenues and the scent of sweetness
thickens the air, somewhere far from
the dust and rot of the workers' quarters
where stools sits stagnant in gutters
and you can smell humans with every
breath—bodies just waiting to die—
that place where the air of cool clean,
roses, violets, geraniums covers everything;
yes, there is nothing else for her to do
but drag that man into the light with
the bright of her big old smile.

Mother Ola and the Poet

sonnet
ab,

He thinks he found me somewhere in his head,
thinks he made me out of nothing much,
just some scraps of dreams on his hot bed,
some discarded conversations like the mulch
of fantasy; but what he doesn't know
is I came to him; he saw me standing
on the corner of one of those slow
summer days, me with a bag, barely moving,
and he stopped, cigarette burning in his lips,
and I let him look until he knew how old
I was, knew what I have seen slip
through two hundred years of this world.
He doesn't know that I am still singing
him home, still drawing him in, just calling.

Stories

The story is an old one, like the predictability
of blood; it will flow and dry if left alone;
it will rush to the surface when the skin
is heated. That old man, the soldier,
would tell of the crushing of skulls,
the rapid chaos of flight, men determined
to see the inert bloody body of their
enemies; the stomach-loosening
rush of fear, the rugged act of muscles
called in to break bones, the sick
soft crack of bones pressed too far,
the tick of a knife slicing flesh,
a knife's feel of the soft give at the
parting of skin and fat and muscle:
and he tells all of this like he
would tell of a ghost rising before
his child's face, there at the door
of the pigeon coop—this barefoot,
white-dressed woman, old as sin,
scowling, her eyes alert though
she has been dead a year, telling
him with a sharp rap on his head—
see the bruise—that he should
set the pigeons free like he promised
his friend he would—another story
of a man quarreling with the wind
and the wind speaking back to him.
And the woman, the girl, the open-
mouthed admirer, feels the rise
of bile in her throat, wants to hold
her face away from the story, and yet
is drawn into these tales, the evidence

in the body of this boy, this man—
and she knows how close death
is because death has come so close
to her, and when we think of death
it's easy to turn to the light of living,
the need for a sudden act of abandon,
and how easily a kiss erupts inside
her body into something so close
to death, so close to the fear
and curse of a story told, a song
sung, a lie, thick with haunting and dread.

Exodus

1904

Nothing will unsettle a man who hires blacks
more than a man who doesn't need hiring,
a thick-necked, dark-suited negro preacher,
calling himself Moses, gathering up the believers
to build that wall around the tabernacle city;
that preacher who can read out God's word
and open his hands wide and clap,
saying, "God is my provider. I work only
for Jesus! He got my pay, come Sunday,
so don't come telling me what to preach!
God is my bossman." That man will tell
his people to pool and buy some land
to build a temple, and soon they are building
schools, and putting up poles for lights
and calling themselves a city, and that
can rile up a white man looking for good
simple workers. Which is how come
they burnt the church to the ground,
how come they told that preacher
to run, how come the congregation
of folks, left with nothing and no
ties but the duty of scrubbing
gravestones, all decided quick
and easy to start walking north, to follow
the thick-necked preacher up that road
to find a plot of land to plant a new
sanctuary, to build a dream. That is how
Martha Pentecost left Alabama behind
her, the dogwoods turning white,
her heart dry as leather, her soul open
only to the hum of Jesus in the wind.

Stillness

When all the talking
is over, she sits
alone in this room

heavy with the scent
of hair grease
and the dull cold

after the fire has gone
down to embers.
She stares down

at the snug fit
of the boards
in the floor she has

polished three days
a week to a soft
glow, old wood giving

in to her push
and circle; she looks
up at the window,

sees a sky crowded
out by the elm's
leaves, and a bird,

a pigeon, hops
from limb to sill,
then quickly

in a darting flutter
is gone. She hears
the sound

of the whistle,
and she feels in that
moment as if home

is too far away,
and flight is too high
a price to pay.

Then she feels
the rock and rumble
of the train in her bones.

Steel

Only when the coals are white with heat,
softening the sheet metal so he can
bend and shape it into tools for
everyday use; only when he can feel
the heat against his groin and stomach
and smell the sweet crisping of his
beard when he is too close; only
there in that backyard backing
up to a dense growth of old-growth
forest before the sudden wall
of the mountain shadowing all;
only there where he can see
the spirit of clouds above,
and the quarreling of birds he
still has no name for; only
then, as sweat beads his head
and he feels the power of the maker
in his hands, does he know
what holy is, does he understand
the language tumbling out of
the round fat black man doing
his jig in the stony yard, pigeon
in his hand, head yanked off,
blood spilling over the few
blades of green scattered
about; only then does he know
what it feels like for people
to wonder out loud, "Is God
in the wind, is he in the river
water, is he in the rain, or is he
there in the fire, constant, silent
as only the fiercest beauty can be?"

What Ola Says

1
Starvation

This enterprise is built on the ingenuity
of starvation. Hunger is the ordering
truth of any good plantation. No mystery
to this. Give one negro something
and the other nothing, and soon a society
is built on need. There are four angels
in the field; run away and you'll see
how quickly black angel will tell
the white man where you went and how
it is the order of starvation. They made
monsters of us; and the red raw
flesh of our betrayals is how they stayed
on top. I sing songs of love, teaching
us a common language, our only healing.

2
1838

> . . . thy rod and thy staff they comfort . . .
> —Psalm 23

It comes to us in whispers and the relay
of news from town to town: somewhere,
negroes like us were waking early
in the morning with no sound of the overseer's
bellow, with no ring of the iron pot
to make them labor to fill the white
man's coffers. Somewhere they have cut

off the draining of blood, the bite
of despair riding us; chattel, slave,
property no more. The English said stop,
let the niggers have their own names;
but here in these states of freedom up
in the righteous North, we must wear the shame
of bondsmen. Is this how wicked God
is? Where, oh love, is Moses's rod?

3
Haiti

They say it was a lie, say it wasn't
men with Africa in their bones who faced
the bayonet, canon and guns bursting
from the phalanx of white soldiers, grey-
faced and troubling. But we heard the news
in the wind of how they sprinted forward,
Yoruba songs in their throats, how they flew
over open fields and turned those cowards
into bloody red carcasses—for freedom;
they stole it, raised it high, frightening
the lie of helplessness we have come
to own. Oh Toussaint, oh brother Boukman,
come up here to Alabama, teach us the words
you used to smash through their evil world.

4
Stono's Ghosts

Here they come, floating in the mist,
floating because their last breaths
were taken, feet dangling, bound-up wrists
pulled at their backs; kicking ugly deaths.

But here they come, dancing through the trees,
ninety-two of them with eyes on fire,
wondering whether that old humming of bees
in their heads saying, "Freedom!" has died
to silence; or whether we made it home
to Spanish Florida before the crossing
to Africa. How to tell them the dumb
gods have stayed silent, all of them sleeping?
How to say the auction block is still warm
with the feet of new slaves facing old storms?

5
A Woman's Curse

Now, women forget all those things they don't want to remember,
and remember everything they don't want to forget.
—Zora Neale Hurston, *Their Eyes Were Watching God*

When you have lost track of years, and only seasons
and the body's changes make sense to you,
it is hard to lie that this woman's remembering
is hers to stop and start as she wants to.
So hard now to conjure up the salt smell
of my mother's skin when she returned weary
from the fields, the melody in the swell
of her voice, deep in the night, to carry
away from me the fear of the siren of insects
and the moaning in the dark forests around us.
I try to return to my tongue the wrecked
language I used to know, but all I have is the rust
of forgetting in me. Sometimes I have prayed
to forget the blood and all I see before me is red.

6
Engine

I know the language of engines; the train
is no stranger to me; we frail humans
took so long to listen to the engine
of the Gods—Ogun with his hot iron,
Shango with his flame. Saw me a motorcar
the other day; made my heart hum and smile
to smell the combustion and see the pure
white smoke of the steam of bitter bile
that has moved me to fly through forests,
blade cutting the wandering fool
who has lost his way. The world's chest
is heaving; that is the music the tools
of the ancestors make, and now they've returned
to teach us how the black earth burns.

7
Sweetness

Some things won't lose their sweetness, it's true:
the wash of light at the back of my neck
when the Holy Spirit comes brightly in view,
and the body, this body, breaks like an insect
drunk with the last spasms of fornicating
before it slips into the wind happy as leaves.
Such sweetness stays on my skin
even when it's drying to a toughness with grief,
because a body doesn't forget its birthing,
the flare of nerves trying to make
flesh from flesh. God gave us these things
between our legs, so ugly they wake

only laughter and shining in you,
to beat back the sad song, to beat back the blues.

8
Book

> They send me to eat in the kitchen . . .
> —Langston Hughes, "I, Too"

It took me one hundred years to read a book
and now I am seeking one hundred years
of what was stolen from me. Those old crooks
stole my language, stole my name, didn't care
that all they gave me was bad feelings
and an ocean of emptiness spread before me.
But what they stole was what was hidden
in those words; they stole a universe, a sea
of stories, worlds and worlds I never knew
could be sitting there beside me, cool,
silent before I could eat up each clue
to the impossible. This is what they stole.
For a hundred years, I will devour it all.
Now watch me growing fat and tall-tall.